F

Bob go write your own.

Ned Roscoe

BAGATORIALS

JOHN ROSCOE & NED ROSCOE

A BOOK FULL OF BAGS

A FIRESIDE BOOK • PUBLISHED BY SIMON & SCHUSTER

FIRESIDE
Rockefeller Center
1230 Avenue of the Americas
New York, NY 10020

FIRESIDE and colophon are registered trademarks of Simon & Schuster Inc.

Designed by Barbara Marks
Illustrated by Robert Leighton, The World's Greatest Cartoonist

Manufactured in the United States of America

2 4 6 8 10 9 7 5 3 1

Library of Congress Cataloging-in-Publication Data
Roscoe, John (John F.)
Bagatorials : a book full of bags / John Roscoe & Ned Roscoe.
p.   cm.
1. Libertarianism—United States.   I. Roscoe, Ned, date.
II. Title.
JC599.U5R63   1996
320.5' 12—dc20   96-14978
CIP

ISBN 0-684-80276-7

Contents

Foreword:
Paper or Plastic?—A Choice, Not an Echo!

by Ian Shoales

A few years back I bought a six-pack of beer from a Cheaper! store in Woodland, California. As I set it on the seat next to me, I suddenly noticed that the brown paper bag in which my purchase had been bundled was emblazoned with, of all things, a headline; it read, in red capital letters an inch high, "CHP RIP OFF ARTISTS." Beneath this bold attention-grabber was a graphic of a highway patrolman (with shades), his hand stuck in a cookie jar. Curious, I started reading the essay, only to find at the bottom of the bag words I don't think I'd ever seen in prose before: "Continued on Side 2."

As I recall, the hard-hitting exposé took all four sides! Flipping the bag over frantically, I managed to absorb a grim tale of Highway Patrol officers allegedly retiring early on disability pensions they don't deserve, in collusion with "whore doctors" and shyster lawyers, to bilk millions from the unwary taxpayer.

Wow! What a story! The reporter even got a byline and a bio. A bag with a byline! I'd never seen anything like it.

I wound up writing a rather snide column about it for the *San Francisco Examiner,* but some enthusiasm for this new prose venue must have leaked through despite myself. Because, while I did receive a certain amount of negative mail on the piece from disgruntled consumers in California's Central Valley ("You suck!"), I was surprised to find an amused letter from the powers-that-be who run Cheaper!, thanking me for paying attention, and sending me a heady collection of their essays, which I was informed are called "bagatorials." (This is one of those words, like "imagineer," or "dramedy," that history will perhaps judge unfortunate, but since they're paying me to write this, I'll stick with it.)

For a while I lived in fear that I might myself become a topic for a bagatorial—SHOALES

GETS FAT ON PUBLIC TROUGH!—but instead, earlier this year, I was invited to write this foreword (forebag?) to the first (and, I hope, not the last) anthology of Cheaper! bagatorials. I'm thrilled to do it. It makes me feel like the Central Valley's answer to Edmund Wilson.

I could let the bagatorials speak for themselves, but (again) since I'm being paid to write a prologue (bagalogue?), I ought to say something.

The headlines, you'll discover, are generally a call for action: DRIVE AND BE FREE! and DECRIMINALIZE DRUGS!

(I like writers who flirt with sedition and are unafraid of exclamation marks.)

And their subject matter fully lives up to the urgency of their banners. Topics range from detailed explications of their legal woes (shades of Lenny Bruce!) to instructions on how to train your child to be a capitalist (blatant propaganda!).

In these pages, you will see that the authors are against taxes, redevelopment, socialized medicine, bad manners, and expensive colas. They want to privatize the state lottery; they say that government is theft ("Consider privatizing everything, including roads, schools, and justice"). They disapprove of price supports for milk, and toll plazas, but they approve of irradiated food and (grudgingly) smoking (your choice, bud).

I should confess that I don't necessarily share all bagatorial opinions. Sure, I disapprove of big government as much as the next guy, but I remain unconvinced that privatizing the post office (say) will make the mail move any faster. I suspect the new competing postal companies would pester me with phone calls around dinnertime urging me to switch my postal service to take advantage of lower rates, the same way the phone companies have done since deregulation. However much we complain about the federal government, at least they never call us up while we're eating to thank us for voting. (Or maybe they do. I answer phone calls at dinnertime with "Leave me alone or I'll kill you!," then slam down the receiver, so I'm not the best one to judge.)

But there's more in these pages than strong opinions. There are book reviews! There are recommendations of books for kids (a very fine list it is too), of self-help books, and literature. In their passionate pursuit of literacy, the folks at Cheaper! will even sell you a copy of *Atlas Shrugged* at below list price, and give you a ten-dollar gift certificate in exchange for your pledge that you've read it. They actually pay you to read Ayn Rand! (That's about the only way I'd ever read her, but they'd have to cough up a lot more than ten bucks.)

You'll also find celebrations of the joys of dining together as a family; you'll learn how to plan a romantic dinner or a kid's birthday party. The question will be answered: what should we expect from the police? You'll find rage at "fat cats," uplifting quotes, homilies, jokes, cries for simple justice!

Beneath every bagatorial are the running themes "Fraud and force are evil, liberty is good, and the nature of man is corruptible." But these are messages tempered by hope: one of the bags has a swell cartoon of a judge, policeman, and Cheaper! clerk gazing sternly, but fairly, toward a new tomorrow.

Some people may prefer coupons for cat litter on their bags. Me, I prefer aphorisms: "We suffer most from the poverty of desire." I prefer sweeping declarations: "Air-quality tyrants choke us worse than ever.""There is no drought."When I'm buying a cold six, I prefer thoughtful essays by Milton Friedman and scholars from the Cato Institute. I like to see those lovely words "More on bottom of bag."

Yes indeedy, as the authors say, "Life is tough on the prairie," life is indeed "nasty, brutish, and short," but the exuberance of the essays makes their Hobbesian philosophy glisten like condensation on an amazingly inexpensive gallon of milk.

What a stroke of genius to put capitalist philosophy on grocery bags! I only regret that you can't experience the essays you are about to read in their natural habitat. Even so, I'm sure you'll find that the prose herein is more than mere bagatelle; it may in fact be the brand-new bag that Papa's got. I hope this is clear.

And I hope these bagatorials catch on. The format could even expand: fiction in serial form (continued on next bag); bag novel—call it a "bagel."Throw in more photos and cartoons: call it a "bagazine."

In the meantime, I'm sure you'll enjoy this collection enormously, even in its booklike format. The prose won't get soggy in the least. On the other hand, you can't put your garbage in it when you're done reading.Well, life is full of hard choices. I'm sure the tough-minded bagatorialists would agree.

Don't Vote!
It Only Encourages Them . . .

by Robert LeFevre

Non-voters will win the election. It's safe to say that half of the population over the age of eighteen will not vote in the coming election. Non-voters will be in the majority and should be declared winners. Check the really important score after the election: how many voted? Few will. If fewer than 30 percent of voting-age adults vote for the winner, shouldn't the election be ignored? There are 185,105,441 adults in the United States. Anything less than 55,531,623 votes is tyranny.

Though we oppose voting on a moral basis (because it's wrong to coerce others), we think as a practical matter that even those who do would agree that candidates should get at least 30 percent of the adult population to vote for them before they take office. If candidates don't poll at least 30 percent of the adult population, the offices should be left vacant.

With this proposal, it would take 30 percent of the adult U.S. population—that's 55,531,623 votes—to take office. It would take 30 percent of the adult California population—or 6,602,788 votes—to elect a senator. Check the vote tallies on November 3 to see if there are any who attain this. Politicians should voluntarily excuse themselves from offices if they do not get this much sanction from their victims. Politicians, we challenge you.

Think about the tremendous difference between what you were taught in Civics and how the system really works. Then think about what a vote for an unsatisfactory candidate means. Think about the absurdity of reducing your opinion on complicated issues to a one-time yea-or-nay. The nonvoters have figured it out. There are better ways to spend time.

Avoid encouraging the abuse of power. Only a few choose the figureheads in America's gigantic governments. This year, as for decades past, the president will be elected by a minority of the population. A vast plurality—perhaps even a majority—will not vote. In 1988, Mr. Bush was supported by only 26 percent of the population. Hardly a mandate.

Self-government is the best of all systems. Most advocate democracy just because it resembles self-government. Americans have fought for self-government and freedom. For years, Americans governed

What It Takes To Get A Mandate		
Location	Adult Population	30%
National	185,105,441*	55,531,623
California	22,009,296*	6,602,789

*U.S. Census, 1990.

themselves. Today, democracy puts a public stamp of approval on a government growing to enormous, stifling proportions. Authoritarians always claim to do the will of the people. Stop being part of the authoritarians' excuse. Stop voting.

Even those who vote admit to choosing the lesser of two evils. Both parties can point to each other's horrendous shortcomings, and justly so. It's really not a case of the lesser of two evils—it's the same evil. No matter how you voted in 1988, you would have gotten tax increases. No matter how you vote in 1992, you're going to get a larger, more intrusive government. The two parties are two peas in a pod. Most politicians are really good buddies with each other. Face it: What your government wants from you is more taxes and more allegiance. It wants you to obey. It wants you to give your consent. It wants you to be politically correct. Instead, we say, concentrate on how you can do good. Turn your attention to those near you.

> I ask no one to sacrifice himself in order to promote my ideas. I demand no allegiance, no taxes, no devotion. I say—free yourself to the best of your ability! The more freedom you obtain for yourself, the more you create for me, for everyone. I would like you to have all that you desire praying at the same that you wish as much for the next man. I urge you to create and to share your creation with those less fortunate. If someone asks you to vote for him at the next election, ask him, I beg you, what he can do for you that you cannot do yourself. Ask him whom he is voting for. If he tells you the truth, then go to the polls and vote for yourself.
>
> —Henry Miller

Some people vote in order to send a message. The message is "Continue business as usual." Any other message is forgotten. After 1964, the peace candidate waged war. In 1972, the law-and-order candidate broke the law. After 1988, Bush's lips read taxes.

Frankly, your vote is statistically insignificant, despite what you've been told. Standard provoting press releases list several elections decided by one vote. Hitler, they say, became the leader of the Nazi Party by one vote. This is ridiculous. No one you know can point to an election in which his or her vote would have been decisive between good and evil. Very, very few can show their vote mattered in a choice between evil and evil. Good things take more work than a single vote. Good things take more effort. And if our vote was the deciding vote: is it right that your choice should mean that 250 million people must have it your way?

Compare our electoral systems with those around the globe. In communist societies, voting is required—so the vote in and of itself is not freedom. In corrupt countries, nonvoting is a potent message of popular discontent. In America, there has been enough personal freedom for people to prosper despite the predations of the political process. Each vote has been a step down the Road to Serfdom.

Think through the theory of voting. Why does might make right? Why is it important

Definitions

majority: . . . A number more than half . . . The political party, group, or faction having the most power by virtue of its larger representation or electoral strength.

plurality: . . . In a contest of more than two alternatives, the number of votes cast for the winning alternative when this number is not more than one half of the total votes cast . . . the larger or greater part of something.

democracy: . . . rule by the majority.

—*American Heritage Dictionary, Second College Edition*

for more people to vote? Does it make the decision better? In 1988, many people voted for president to keep taxes from increasing. If more people had voted for Bush, would he have kept his word? If more people voted for Dukakis, would he have changed his position and opposed higher taxes?

Candidates, we know, are undependable. It's not just that they tend to be bad people, although they do tend to be bad people. Even good people faced with the temptations of being in public office will become corrupt. Ballot initiatives are no better. Search through the history of any ballot initiative and you'll see a scheming, plotting special interest, angling for its own advantage. Questions are carefully crafted and buried in verbiage so that every answer is wrong. Most answers depend on a mystical belief that yes, all is for the best in this, the best of all possible worlds. There's a civic religion out there, cynically manipulated by the powerful to be the opiate of the masses. Civics teachers are the evangelists. Just say Don't.

Go find your Civics teacher and challenge the theory. How can one vote, you might ask, in order to reduce government spending? How can one vote in order to restore personal freedom? How can one vote for freedom of education? How can one vote for free trade in the California milk business? Many taxes will be paid, many school days spent, many gallons purchased before the ideal candidate is elected, before that necessary ballot proposition passes. Should government even be involved in many of its activities? Hardly. Should you participate in the process and in doing so give your sanction? No.

. . . all experience hath shewn, that mankind are more disposed to suffer, while evils are sufferable, than to right themselves by abolishing the forms to which they are accustomed.
—*Declaration of Independence*

Yes, if you don't vote, you can still comment. Look at us. In fact, you can comment on the truly important aspects of living. Our advice? Ask not what you can say at the ballot box. Ask what you can do to live your own life better. Then do it. Do the right thing in your own affairs. Solve your own troubles. Avoid being part of the problem. If you work for the

Don't Vote: 20 Practical Reasons

1. You know the present political system doesn't work. You know it doesn't make a difference who wins. It won't make a difference who wins. It won't make a difference to you.
2. You don't believe the majority is always right. Your parents told you the truth when they said they didn't care what the other kids did, you ought to do what's right on your own.
3. You think the government has your name on enough pieces of paper.
4. You don't want to give any candidate the idea that he or she represents you.
5. You think all candidates are lying.
6. You believe you are victimized by politics and politicians. You don't want to give the sanction of the victim to any politician.
7. You think it's immoral to impose your view on others. You believe the best course of action will be decided by individuals without government interference.
8. You think the candidates would say anything, promise anything, and do anything to get elected.
9. You believe power corrupts and absolute power corrupts absolutely. You believe incumbent politicians attain absolute power.
10. You want to send a message to politicians that government isn't the most important thing in your life and you are not going to waste your time voting.
11. You have something better to do with your time on November 3, 1992.
12. You want to join the 75 percent of American adults who won't vote for the next President of the United States.
13. You don't think political parties represent ideologies. You think the parties are a collection of people who combine to attain power over others.
14. You don't have an intelligent or logical reason to vote. You prefer to act in ways that make sense to you.
15. You know the incumbent almost always wins. You don't think it's in your best interest to add to the power of politicians.
16. You don't believe in the Civic Religion. You don't worship this way.
17. You didn't register. You want to avoid jury duty.
18. You don't believe what they told you in high school Civics. The system doesn't work as they said it would. Since they were wrong about the system, they were almost certainly wrong about the good voting does.
19. You don't want to give government any reason to get bigger, or to legitimize it. You think the 44 percent of the Gross National Product they now spend is enough.
20. You think nonvoting makes a bigger statement than voting.

DON'T VOTE!

government, quit. If you're on welfare, get off. Develop your personal freedom by earning more. Maintain your personal freedom by respecting the rights of others. Do unto others as you would have them do unto you. Respect the boundaries of others. Be a good example. Don't vote.

Check the participation numbers after Election Day. Most people already got the message.

How decisions will be made:

Frankly, we don't have a grand plan. We have specific plans for our own lives and our own business. Everybody would be better off to work on accomplishing one's own specific plan with due respect to others. Some of you will write to us to tell us our ulterior purpose is to help that womanizing, draft-dodging, dope-smoking, tax-and-spend opportunist. Those who think they understand business expect us to secretly support the wimpy, war-mongering, tax-and-spend incumbent who lied to the American people. Even the autarchic, buzz-cut, tax-but-don't-spend corporate fascist has no attraction for us. No, none of the above. You know what we'll do on Election Day? Sell milk Cheaper!

Reasons to Vote

1. Get off work early.
2. Get out of doing tasks for spouse.
3. Your parents told you to vote.
4. Protect your patronage job.
5. To avoid feeling guilty.
6. Your spouse nags you to vote.
7. Your employer pressures you to vote.
8. You get a monetary gain from the results.
9. Television tells you to vote.
10. You dislike someone so much you vote for his or her opponent.
11. You worry about what will happen to society if you don't vote.
12. It shows you have an opinion.
13. If you couldn't vote, you'd be outraged.
14. You want to show you speak English.
15. You can meet friends and neighbors at the polling place and discuss affairs and do business.
16. Walking a mile to the polls is good for your health.
17. One can announce to friends smugly, "I've already voted."
18. You may meet Elvis at the polls.

1992 Primary Results	LOCATION	ADULT POPULATION	VOTED
	New York	13,730,906*	974,509
	California	22,009,296*	4,842,537

% VOTED NEW YORK 7.1%	% VOTED CALIFORNIA 22%	NO MANDATE!

*U.S. Census, 1990.

Abstain from Beans

by Robert LeFevre

In ancient Athens, those who admired the Stoic philosophy of individualism took as their motto: "Abstain from Beans." The phrase had a precise reference. It meant: DON'T VOTE. To vote in Athens one dropped various-colored beans into a receptacle.

To vote is to express a preference. There is nothing implicitly evil in choosing. All of us in the ordinary course of our daily lives vote for or against dozens of products and services. When we vote for (buy) any good or service, it follows that by salutary neglect we vote against the goods or services we do not choose to buy. The great merit of marketplace choosing is that no one is bound by any other person's selection. I may choose Brand X. But this cannot prevent you from choosing Brand Y.

When we place voting into the framework of politics, however, a major change occurs. When we express a preference politically, we do so precisely because we intend to bind others to our will. Political voting is the legal method we have adopted and extolled for obtaining monopolies of power. Political voting is nothing more than the assumption that might makes right. There is a presumption that any decision wanted by the majority of those expressing a preference must be desirable, and the inference even goes so far as to presume that anyone who differs from a majority view is wrong or possibly immoral.

But history shows repeatedly the madness of crowds and the irrationality of majorities. The only conceivable merit relating to majority rule lies in the fact that if we obtain monopoly decisions by this process, we will coerce fewer persons than if we permit the minority to coerce the majority. But implicit in all political voting is the necessity to coerce some so that all are controlled. The direction taken by the control is academic. Control as a monopoly in the hands of the state is basic.

In times such as these, it is incumbent upon free men and women to reexamine their most cherished, long-established beliefs. There is only one truly moral position for an honest person to take. He must refrain from coercing his fellows. This means that he should refuse to participate in the process by means of which some men obtain power over others. If you value your right to life, liberty, and property, then clearly there is every reason to refrain from participating in a process that is calculated to remove the life, liberty, or property from any other person. Voting is the method for obtaining legal power to coerce others.

Neither Ballots nor Bullets!

by Carl Watner

America's most powerful polling booth is the cash register. There's a vote that really counts.

When you make a purchase at a Cheaper! store, you make us a little bit stronger. It's a vote for us over our competition. Choices are made and lives are changed by the decisions you make while shopping.

Think how this differs from the government polls. The government asks you to vote occasionally. If your choice loses, tough luck. You're bound to live by the results. If the whole process turns you off, tough luck. You have no choice but to deal with the government. If they pass a law, you have to obey it. If they demand a tax, you have to pay it. Then, to add insult to injury, they tell you that what they're doing is "the will of the people."

Where Are the Real Elections?

With us, you have a choice. You can vote every day in hundreds of different ways. In our stores, you have plenty of choices. (Soda or beer? Pepsi, Coke, or It'sa Cola? Some of each?) If you don't like our store, you can go to a lot

of other places, or you can decide not to shop at all. If we raise prices, you can tell us we're crazy and you can go somewhere else.

Those products that you buy and the places at which you shop prosper. Those that you ignore tend to wither away. The more you spend, the bigger and stronger the business becomes. When the business gets so big and proud that it stops caring about getting your vote, quality suffers—and you can take your business else-where.

After the shopping-election is over, our stores give you value for money. You can take the purchase home and enjoy it. After the political election, what do you have? Promises?

Plus, your shopping-vote comes with a money-back guarantee. Try doing that with your vote at the polls! The government would suffer moral bankruptcy! Think of the returns Nixon and Carter would have had!

You Are a Self-Governor

The economic marketplace is all about self-government. You govern your own life. You make choices about when to get up, what to eat, how to budget your money, where to live, and what to do. The majority doesn't decide this for you. This is how millions of people live together in peace and prosperity.

When the government steps in, things are thrown out of whack. Every day, the government becomes more involved in our daily lives. Only more self-government and less political government will get us moving in the right direction again. After all, what can the government do that you and I, or voluntary groups of us, can't do? Fight wars? Collect taxes? Maybe those things shouldn't be done anyway.

Some cry, "But the government has to pay for such-and-such." Where does all the government's wealth come from? From you and me and all the other millions of people who produce it daily. The government possesses no magical powers to create wealth.

You Can Make a Difference

If we live honestly and assume the responsibility of caring for ourselves and our families, we have no need for the ballot box. This quiet way of changing society is nonviolent and apolitical. We each labor in our own garden, doing our best to present society with an improved product: ourselves. Focus on making yourself better as an individual. Don't waste your time waiting for everyone else to become better as a group. As individuals improve, the improvement of society will take care of itself. You are the key to a better world.

Well, what do you think? Write to us at: Cheaper!, P.O. Box 886, Benicia, CA 94510.

Taxation Is Theft!

Your money belongs to you. Governments have no money of their own.
Who pays taxes voluntarily? What's yours is yours. You should be able to spend your own money as you see fit. To take it from you is theft. The only money the government has is what it takes from you and me. Does the government own everything you worked for? Not in America!

Pay Your Taxes Anyway

Even with a polite, formal institutional process, stealing is stealing. Coercion is coercion. That's why taxation is theft. No purpose justifies it. (You must pay your taxes, however, or else face horrible consequences.)

It's not just government waste that bothers us. Too much government bothers us. America is rich and prosperous, so we don't mind a little clip here and there, especially if it's in the public interest. Roads, schools, national defense, and care of the poor are all good things. A combination of private initiative and public direction have made things work out pretty well in the past. Unfortunately, the government's slice of the pie is getting so big that it ruins everything. The American government now spends 44 percent of the national income. That is too much.

Is Government the Only Way?

People forget that it's possible to achieve the goals of good society through individual enterprise and voluntary contributions. To say that the governmental process is the only way to protect, educate, and feed the country is silly, but many people agree with that statement. To think that these difficult tasks can be accomplished best by organizations notorious for inefficiency and corruption is crazy, but many people can't imagine any other method.

No, it's not the method of taxation that we find objectionable. The American tax system is quite clever. Most taxes are collected with a little grumbling, but everybody pays. It would be better if the system were simpler, but at least, if you pay your taxes, they leave you alone for a while.

You Should Be Free

That's the principle of the matter. We think people ought to be free to spend their own money the way they see fit. No matter what they teach in school, that isn't the way it works here. Sure, those with fat pockets and powerful friends may win some tax breaks, but the average citizen, even if he's a dedicated voter, can't have any effect on the system. For most of us, the government makes demands as if we were owned by the government.

We pay our taxes. There really isn't a choice. We have no intention of becoming tax martyrs. Nor do we know of any good reason to lie or cheat in order to reduce the size of the taxman's bite. But there is something you can do. . . .

Just Say No!

If you object to taxes, don't take money from the government. Don't be part of the problem. If you think something ought to be done, make a plan to do it—using funds freely invested and contributed. Persuade people to help you.

If the government offers you a payment, a subsidy, a grant, a guarantee, a job, or a handout, just say no. It's tough, but you never get something for nothing. What the government gives you, they take from someone else. It isn't theirs to give. Taxes are evil. You should try to be good.

This bag is a message about self-reliance and freedom. If you have comments or questions, please write to us at: Cheaper!, P.O. Box 886, Benicia, CA 94510.

We Believe

by Wendy McElroy

"Man is free at the moment he wishes to be."
—*Voltaire*

You are a self-owner. You own your body. This is an inescapable truth of human nature: you and you alone control your actions and are responsible for them.

The alternative is that someone else owns your body, which is slavery.

Your labor is a direct extension of your body. As such, you own the profits of your labor. Whatever you produce is your property, in the same sense that your body is your property.

The alternative is slavery.

Every other human being is also a self-owner. It is wrong to use force against anyone, because this violates their self-ownership; it violates their rights.

By using force you tell other people that you have a right to control their bodies and their property. You say that they are less than human beings.

Government law is just a form of force that some people—called legislators—have agreed on.

Laws don't change anything. People don't need the law to tell right from wrong.

When men are pure, laws are useless;
when men are corrupt, laws are broken.
—*Benjamin Disraeli*

A peaceful society comes from respecting each other's boundaries. This is a compassionate society where people lend the other fellow a helping hand.

Force kills the natural compassion people feel for each other. Force is the death of humane society.

The absence of force will not bring utopia.

Utopia is not possible on earth. But freedom offers the best chance we have for happiness and prosperity. Freedom is the best we can do.

Doesn't Freedom Mean Doing Anything You Want?

No. Liberty does not mean license. It means self-government. Freedom has obligations. The two main ones are:

1. You must take responsibility for yourself and for your actions. You can't blame others for what's wrong. Take control of your own life.
2. You must respect the freedom of other people. It is wrong to use force or fraud. Force denies people's humanity. Fraud denies the truth.

> When a . . . man governs himself, that is self-government; but when he governs himself and also governs another man, that is despotism. . . . No man is good enough to govern another man without that other's consent.
> —*Abraham Lincoln*

But What of Government?

Government is just a group of people who claim the right to tell you what to do with your life. They get away with this because they are "elected." According to politicians, this means that a majority has voted them into office. In fact, less than 50 percent of Americans voted for *anyone* in the last elections.

Even if a majority had elected them, what would it matter? Why should you obey? Might doesn't make right.

If it is wrong for one man to take your money, how can it be right for a group of men? Calling it "taxes" rather than "theft" doesn't change the fact—it is *your* money.

Anything that is wrong for an individual to do is wrong for a group of individuals.

Government gets away with force because it claims to "represent the people." Politicians represent their own interest. Government exists to benefit its members—politicians, bureaucrats, and other people who can't get an honest job. They grow fat off you and your family.

> As long as I count the votes, what are you going to do about it?
> —*William Marcy (Boss) Tweed, nineteenth-century New York politician*

All organizations exist to serve their members. This is also true of businesses. But business is voluntary. No one is forced to buy or sell. An exchange occurs only if both sides think they benefit. The only choice government gives you is: pay up or go to jail.

Customers vote with their dollars. If a businessman stops caring about your vote, you can take your dollars elsewhere. What choice do you have with a politician? Will he give you a money-back guarantee? Can you take your business elsewhere?

Why Are You So Against Government?

Government produces nothing. It operates through force and fraud. It takes money from you and your family. It makes promises it does not keep.

Politicians steal your freedom. Then they insult your intelligence by asking for your vote.

Government destroys people's independence through its promises to take care of them. But how many people can trust Social Security to support them in old age? How many people are homeless because they believed in social programs? The government's promises are lies. You have to take care of yourself.

> It is error alone which needs support of government. Truth can stand by itself.
> —*Thomas Jefferson*

Government is the biggest threat to your freedom and safety. It is the biggest threat to your family and friends.

And it keeps growing. . . .

How Much Government Would You Accept?

About the amount that would fit into Independence Hall in Philadelphia. About the amount envisioned by the Founding Fathers.

> A wise and frugal government, which shall restrain men from injuring one another, which shall leave them otherwise free to regulate their own pursuits of industry and improvement, and shall not take from the mouth of labor the bread it has earned—this is the sum of good government.
> —*Thomas Jefferson*

We believe in a night-watchman style of government. A government that acts like a security officer, who patrols a building at night to make sure everything is safe.

A night-watchman government has three functions:
1. to defend against attack (military)
2. to ensure a peaceful society (police)
3. to adjudicate disputes (courts)

It does not tell people how to live. It does not regulate business. It does not provide services, such as the post office or National Arts Council.

What About Essential Government Programs?

> The good governor should have a broken leg and keep at home.
> —*Cervantes*

Most of what government does is not essential. Most is better left undone. For example, your security does not require the U.S. to police the globe. Your family does not need a government-funded space program. Or grants to the arts. Or subsidies to business.

Essential services include roads, postal delivery, medical care, and education. These were provided by the free market until government monopolized them.

Government should never provide essential services. Government is inefficient and corrupt. It leaves the customer—you—with no recourse. If you refuse to pay for bad service, it takes your property.

> Were we directed from Washington when to sow and when to reap, we should soon want bread.
> —*Thomas Jefferson*

People have been brainwashed to think that only government can build a road or deliver a letter. But government doesn't provide any service. Individuals do the work. Individuals pay the bill. Government provides bureaucrats to supervise what the free market would do naturally.

There is a solution: privatize government services. Let the free market do what it does best—provide service.

People forget—before government took over, individuals took care of themselves and others. Literacy rates in colonial New England were higher than they are now. America was crisscrossed by privately built railways. The Pony Express went where no government delivery was attempted.

It is crazy to turn over things like medical care to a bureaucracy. Do you want the

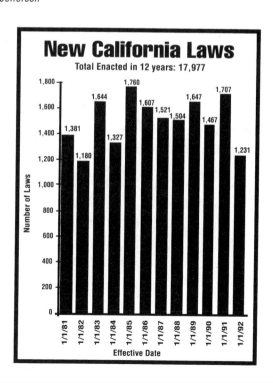

New California Laws

Total Enacted in 12 years: 17,977

same people who run the post office to supervise open-heart surgery? Do you want your life to depend on a civil servant?

The free market can provide society's needs. You can take care of yourself.

What Would a Free Market Society Look Like?

Capitalist acts between consenting adults.

Absolute liberty for the peaceful individual.

A return to the ideals of 1776:

> We hold these truths to be self-evident, that all men are created equal, that they are endowed by their Creator with certain unalienable Rights, that among these are Life, Liberty and the pursuit of Happiness. That to secure these rights, Governments are instituted among Men, deriving their just powers from the consent of the governed.
>
> —*Thomas Jefferson, Declaration of Independence*

So ... What Can I Do About It?

- Never use force or fraud.
- Take control of your life.
- You don't have to lecture people or convert anyone. The solution lies inside yourself.
- Find ways to avoid what government calls "services."
- Educate your children at home or at private schools.
- Provide for your own retirement.
- Volunteer time to a private charity.
- Do someone a good turn ... BUT start with your own family and friends. And make sure you are using your own money and efforts.
- Set a good example. Refuse all forms of government aid. The government doesn't have any money of its own. Whatever it offers, it has to steal. Don't sanction this theft by accepting the bones it throws you.

How Else Can I Change Things?

There is something you should *not* do.

Politics is the problem. Government takes power and dignity from the individual. It steals money. It is a criminal process. Do not become part of the problem.

Do not run for office.

Do not pay homage to public officials. Never contribute your time, money, or approval to a candidate or a political movement.

DO NOT VOTE. Don't willingly surrender control of your life to someone else.

People think they can cast "protest" votes. But you can't attack government by voting. You can't attack crime by becoming an accessory.

Politicians of every stripe tell you to "get out and vote." Because they want your sanction. It is how politicians justify their power over you.

Voting is the way the majority tells the minority how they have to live.

No one has a right to vote on how you live your life. Every vote cast denies your liberty.

> Elector: one who enjoys the sacred privilege of voting for the man of another man's choice.
>
> Vote: the instrument and symbol of a freeman's power to make a fool of himself and a wreck of his country.
>
> —Ambrose Bierce

What Can I Read to Learn More?

These are some of the books we recommend:

Atlas Shrugged, Ayn Rand (the classic novel of individuals challenging authority).

Walden, Henry David Thoreau (a man's quest for self-sufficiency and self-knowledge).

How I Found Freedom in an Unfree World, Harry Browne ("how-to" live free, even under the shadow of the state).

Economics in One Lesson, Henry Hazlitt (the free market explained simply and elegantly).

A Parting Thought

Whatever crushes individuality is despotism, by whatever name it may be called.
—*John Stuart Mill, On Liberty*

The world will never be perfect.

We don't have all the answers. We don't even have all the questions. That's why we want to hear what you think. Write to us. What do you believe?!!

Too Many Taxes

What the Government gives it must first take away.

—*John S. Coleman**

Government spending accounts for close to half of the national income. No one knows the full story, because deficits, off-budget programs, guarantees, special funds, and other accounting tricks make it practically impossible to total it up.

Government officials are much more conscientious when they collect taxes than they are when they spend taxes. If we got our money's worth, who would complain? Taxes are the price paid for civilization, says the Establishment. We doubt it. Most taxes are wasted.

The state of California collected $44.4 billion in 1992–93. The current state budget calls for $56 billion in state spending. That's an impressive increase. What will we get for it?

Federal tax collections in California are $117,352,486,000 higher than when we started business in 1964. In 1964, federal tax collections in California were only $10,443,242,000. State taxes have increased by more than eleven times. Local taxes are over six times higher. The increase in total taxes for 1989-90 is as much as the *total* tax take for 1964–65.

Total federal, state, and local tax collections in California for 1964–65 were $17,543,612,000. Adjusted for inflation between 1964 and 1989, this $17-billion figure would have been $73,332,298,000 on June 30, 1990, at the end of the 1989–90 fiscal year. Assume that this $73-billion inflation-adjusted tax total increased directly in proportion to population growth. Tax collections in California in 1989–90 would have been $118,227,000,000, since California's population increased by 61 percent.

*Former chairman of the Federal Reserve Bank of Chicago.

Instead, total tax collections in California in 1989–90 were $194,833,514,000. Per person, adjusted for inflation, taxes collected in California have increased about 70 percent since 1964.

California's population has increased by 11,037,000, a 61.2 percent increase since we opened our first store in 1964. There are 110,693 more California state employees than in 1964. That's a 76.9 percent increase. California state-tax revenue increased by $40,889,360,000 since 1964. That's a 1,147 percent increase!

> Noah must have taken into the Ark two taxes, one male and one female. And did they multiply bountifully! Next to guinea pigs, taxes must have been the most prolific animals.
> —Will Rogers

> Last year, the State's 58 counties collected nearly $15 billion in property tax revenues. The passage of Proposition 13 in 1978 drastically altered the way in which properties were assessed for tax purposes. This amendment limits the property tax to one percent of taxable value and places a cap of no more than 2% on annual increases. It allows real property to be appraised at its current market value if there is a change in ownership or new construction.

> As a result of the passage of Proposition 13, county property tax revenues fell by 52% in one year, declining from $10.3 billion in 1977–78 to $5.04 billion in 1978-79. Fiscal year 1986–87 marked the first year in which property tax revenues exceeded those collected before the passage of Proposition 13. The figures indicate that county property tax revenues have increased at an average annual rate of 9.8% in the last three fiscal years.
> —State Board of Equalization Annual Report, p. 27

Using the net-taxable and the average property-tax rate for 1990, the counties collected $16,489,326,000 in property taxes in 1990–91. This is an increase in property taxes of $1,769,108,000 or 12.01 percent for 1990–91.

Businessmen say, "All expenses walk on two legs." The average state employee costs over $49,000, including salary, pension, and benefits. Over a quarter of the total state tax collections for 1989–90 went to pay state employees. Local taxes collected in 1989–90 were 300 percent higher than in the first year of Proposition 13. Local taxes are 176 percent of the amount collected the year before Proposition 13 went into effect.

Don't believe a statistic unless you make it up yourself. We've looked at a lot of figures. We've talked to people who compute, tabulate, massage, guess, and borrow numbers. None of the numbers are reliable. Agencies agree on the numbers only when they've taken another source's figures without question. Government is big and complicated. Everyone keeps the numbers differently. If you disagree with our numbers or our interpretation of the numbers, write us a letter and set us straight.

The state Board of Equalization reported 898,222 sales-tax permits in 1989–90. They conducted 21,048 audits. Chances of an audit are two in a hundred. Cheaper! stores are audited every year. That's common for a business that collects a lot of sales tax. About 14.8 percent of our revenues go directly to taxes. Add in income taxes, gas taxes, and excise taxes and it's a lot higher.

Government is much worse than organized crime. We've been in business for twenty-seven years, and in that time we've never met anyone in the "Mafia." On the other hand, we're extorted every day by government officials.

People do good because they want to do good. People obey laws when the laws seem to be the right thing to do. Look at what works. Is it the DMV? Is it the post office? Do the police really keep you from harm? Does welfare cure poverty? The things that work well are the things people choose to spend money on voluntarily. The best government is self-control.

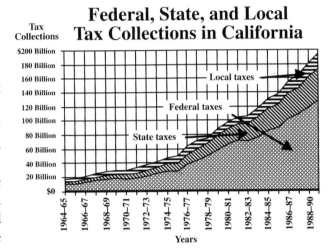

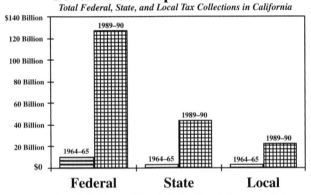

Source: California State Board of Equalization Annual Report for 1989–90. Schedule A-48

Figure out the taxes you pay. Add up the federal and state income taxes and local property taxes. If you're a renter, realize that the landlord charges you for property taxes in the rent. Add 8 percent to your annual purchases to get what you spend on sales taxes. Include the hidden sales tax on gasoline. If you drink alcoholic beverages, drive a car, or smoke cigarettes, guess at the excise taxes. Then figure out the percentage of your family's income that goes to taxes. Talk about that number. Chances are you'll be outraged.

Be part of the solution. If you work for the government, find another job. If you're on the dole, get off. Does your job depend on government contracts? Do you get a monthly check from the government? At least be honest about the source of your income. Do you live off taxes? Would the rest of us volunteer to pay you what you earn? If the answer's no, realize that you're part of the problem.

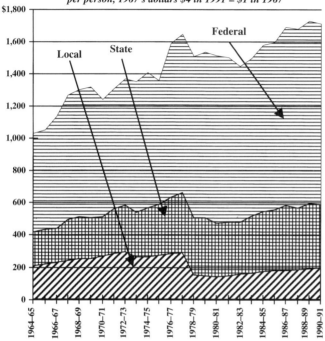

California Taxes
Adjusted for Population and Inflation
per person, 1967's dollars $4 in 1991 = $1 in 1967

Local   State   Federal

It's time to speak up. Talk to the people you work with. Write a letter to the editor. Call a talk show. Be candid with people who work for the government. How's the quality of the service you get from the government? Ask them what it costs. Government functions—schools, roads, charity, crime prevention, mail delivery, bank insurance, etc.—ought to be privatized. It's time to say so.

California State Taxes Explode

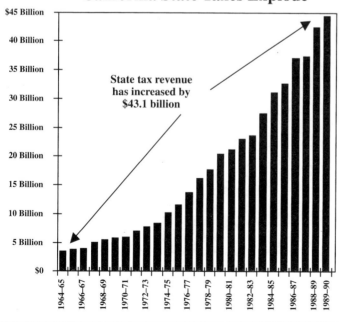

State tax revenue has increased by $43.1 billion

Official California Tax Collections

Tax Year	Federal	State	Local and Ad Valorum
1989–90	$127,795,725	$44,452,225	$22,585,561
1988–89	118,853,725	42,476,369	20,318,188
1987–88	108,332,416	37,507,952	18,435,268
1986–87	101,445,372	37,150,402	16,786,547
1985–86	89,604,350	32,756,530	15,638,373
1984–85	85,348,500	31,191,916	14,325,179
1983–84	76,623,643	27,546,937	12,972,704
1982–83	70,893,434	23,762,901	11,630,998
1981–82	71,541,870	23,081,477	10,527,278
1980–81	67,149,915	21,290,825	9,369,680
1979–80	58,873,061	20,558,664	8,525,000
1978–79	49,558,113	17,781,295	7,515,000
1977–78	42,772,775	16,266,712	12,791,000
1976–77	37,997,043	13,873,801	11,442,000
1975–76	28,091,997	11,661,724	10,093,000
1974–75	28,510,065	10,350,879	9,087,000
1973–74	24,959,348	8,503,309	8,141,345
1972–73	21,386,204	7,859,022	8,150,000
1971–72	18,962,545	7,086,506	7,325,000
1970–71	17,629,909	5,979,962	6,545,000
1969–70	18,596,235	5,851,911	5,789,464
1968–69	16,777,444	5,599,729	5,369,543
1967–68	15,455,808	5,090,195	4,787,145
1966–67	13,098,149	3,978,106	4,336,397
1965–66	11,085,100	3,889,945	3,896,042
1964–65	10,443,242	3,562,865	3,537,505

California Property Tax Levies
The Effect of Proposition. 13 - 1976/77 to 1989/90

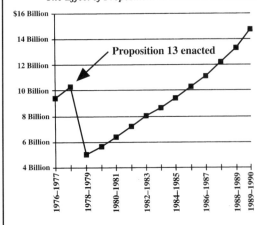

The Number of California State Employees
Grows Faster Than the Population

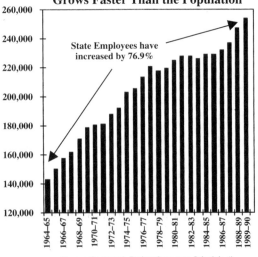

Source: Governor's Budget Summary, Schedule 4b

Read Our Lips:
No New Taxes!

Cheaper! stores sell more for less. We sell satisfaction-guaranteed food and packaged goods for everyday low prices.

We operate in over fifty different cities and towns. Over 40 percent of the dollars we collect go directly to the government in taxes. Three taxes alone—gasoline, cigarette, and sales taxes—are 23 percent of the sales. In some stores, we have two bulletin boards to display all the permits we must have to do what we do.

We write messages on our bags to help our customers and ourselves. Government causes you to pay too much for food. Government causes you to pay too much for fuel. Government causes you to pay too much for housing. If we can help persuade people to oppose the growth of government, we can help our customers keep what they own, and keep what they earn.

We believe in individual action. We believe you should treat other people as you would like to be treated. We believe that if you want to be healthy, you should do what makes sense all the time. If you want to be safe, be careful. If you want to be rich, save your money. If you want to get ahead, work. If you want good done, do it.

We believe many of the rules we live under are wrong, yet we believe you should follow the rules. We know most of the stories written in the newspaper are erroneous, yet we are avid readers. We never believe a number we didn't make up on our own, yet we believe numeracy is essential. We believe that the truth well told is exciting.

We live in a time when the best political position is very simple:

No New Government !
No New Taxes!

Government in the United States spends over 44 percent of our Gross National Product. Most of this money is wasted. This money is spent in ways no sensible person would ever choose. Inefficiency, bureaucracy, and corruption are typical of every government activity.

In addition, government laws, regulations, and restrictions require consumers and businesses to spend a good share of their non-tax dollars in unproductive ways. We all live poorer because of government.

Politicians and bureaucrats think more laws and more money will help government to solve more problems. This has not worked in practice. Welfare makes people poorer. The post office obstructs communication. The FDA obstructs procedures that would make food safer. Local planning leads to blight. Police officers act like the toughest gang in town. California has more prisoners per capita than most of the world, more than at any time in the past, yet criminal behavior is more common.

The government has no money of its own. It only has what it takes from you and me. Unless you pay taxes voluntarily, taxation is theft. You own yourself. You own what you earn to sustain yourself and your family. Most of the good things that happen in society are done voluntarily by individuals. Do the decent thing.

If you work for the government, quit. If you're on the dole, get off. If you sell to the government, stop selling. If you buy from the government, stop buying. Refuse to flatter officials. When people talk about trouble, remind them . . .

No New Government !
No New Taxes!

California's budget grows and grows. Time to shout:

Government Is Theft!

In good times and in bad, California's state government remains faithful to its first love: spending other people's money. The government doesn't care that the state is in the worst economic slump since the Great Depression. It doesn't matter to officials that in two years 800,000 jobs have disappeared[1] and, with them, 800,000 taxpayers.

The politicians and bureaucrats hear the news and shrug their shoulders. All it means is that they'll have to reach deeper into your pockets. And they will. Nothing is going to stop them from spending more.

For four years now, huge budget deficits have plagued the state. The governor and legislature have responded by inflicting a long series of "painful cuts" on state government. Then, after all the trimming, the budget is fatter than ever—and the taxpayers have been skinned.

The last time a California governor proposed a budget that was smaller—1 percent smaller—than the previous year was in 1981. The governor was Jerry M. Brown, the founding father of the Church of Lowered Expectations. Jerry was in the middle of his "smaller-is-better" phase as he prepared to leave office and, as usual, no one was quite sure what, if anything, he had in mind.

Now Pete Wilson is trying the same thing, but everyone knows what's in Pete's mind. Wilson's $51.2-billion budget for 1993–94[2]—11 percent smaller than this year's—might look revolutionary. It's a mirage. Wilson is the least revolutionary of politicians. He's not trying to smash the status quo. He's just trying to hold on to his job. Pete hasn't done anything except take a government paycheck since the 1960s. Now his livelihood is in danger.

Unfortunately for Pete, the Democrats in the legislature want to hold on to their jobs, too. So his budget is doomed. Democrats keep their constituents happy by spending more.

Wilson wants to let a half-cent of the sales tax die, as scheduled, on July 1. Democrats want to extend the tax, even though they promised in 1991 that the tax increase would end this year. That was then, this is now, and political promises have a notoriously short shelf life.

"As the Capitol Churns"

So here we go again in another episode of the great budget soap opera. For the next six or eight months, the governor, the legislature, and the bureaucracy will sob about the deficit. They'll cut and cut and cut the budget, just as they have the past four years. Care to guess what will happen?

Our guess is that the state will wind up spending more and taxing more. Some of the damage may be hidden in obscure taxes on businesses, taxes that businesses pass on in the form of higher prices. Spending increases will be disguised by "overly optimistic" assumptions.

Last summer, after the longest budget crisis in the state's history, in the middle of the worst recession in California since the Great Depression, the state wound up with a 1992–93 budget that called for spending $436 million more than the year before.[3] This might seem like big money to you. It's small change for the people who spend your money in Sacramento.

More important, it's a lie. Now the budget experts tell us that state spending will actually increase by $2.5 billion this year.[4] Somehow, the "overly optimistic" budget cutters made an error of $2 billion last summer.

Don't get excited. In 1991, at the end of another round of big budget "cuts," they increased state spending by $5.5 billion.

Government just keeps growing. It's the nature of the beast.

The state budget is like the mythical creature Hydra. When Hercules cut off one of the monster's nine heads, two grew back in its place. In the past ten years, California state budgets have been cut again and again—and grown larger and larger. Spending has more than doubled: from $26.8 billion in the 1983–84 fiscal year to $57.4 billion for 1992–93.[5]

Never-Enough Budgeting Is Too Much

How can it happen? How can they keep on cutting and cutting—and still spend more and more? The secret lies in the story of a man and his fourteen-year-old daughter. This was back in the days when a dollar was worth a dollar—or at least worth eighty cents.

"Dad," the girl complained one day at the beginning of a new school year, "you cut my allowance by three dollars."

The man looked puzzled. "What do you mean?" he said. "You were getting ten dollars and I raised it to twelve. That's two dollars more."

"But I was planning on getting fifteen," the girl explained slowly and carefully, "and twelve dollars is three dollars less than fifteen. So you cut it three dollars."

"Oh," the man said. His head began to swim as he searched for the words to explain it to the kid. "Forget it," he told himself. "Even if she understands it, she won't like it. She's got her own system of math."

So he invoked his parental authority. "Sorry," he said. "That's all I can afford." With that, the crisis ended.

The teenager and California's governing elite share the same attitude about money. The state budget cuts are just like the kid's allowance cuts. The cuts exist only in the eye of the beholder.

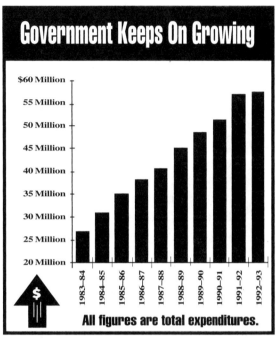

Government Keeps On Growing

All figures are total expenditures.

The state, of course, does it all on a grander scale. Instead of dreaming of a fifteen-dollar allowance, the state budget makers dream in the billions. Last year, they wanted to spend $68.1 billion[6]—$11.1 billion more than the year before. With 10 percent of California's working people unemployed, the budget makers wanted to increase government spending by nearly 20 percent.

This was the great budget "gap" of 1992—the distance between the dreams of the spenders and the reality of the world. It's the same type of fictitious gap the teenager complained about when she didn't get the fifteen-dollar allowance.

In gentler times, the governing class would have closed the "gap" by reaching deeper into the pockets of the governed and pulling out a few billion dollars in new taxes. Last year, those pockets were empty. The taxpayers had their own budget crisis, with state and local taxes already gobbling up, on average, $10,648 a year out of the budget of a family of four.[7]

So the budget makers gave up on their dreams of $11.1 billion. They reluctantly decided to spend only $436 million more than they did the previous year. That, of course, turned into $2.5 billion, but what's a billion or two among friends?

What California needs is what the girl with the allowance had: someone who can listen patiently and then say "No!"

Same Old Scenario: The Crime That Pays

Californiaʼs endless budget "crisis" has become so familiar that politicians and bureaucrats would be lost without it.

Details vary a bit each year, but the scenario remains the same:

- First the politicos discover a budget "gap."
- Then they gasp with astonishment. Devastation is predicted.
- The finger-pointing begins. Accusations of incompetence, of overspending, of callous disregard for the disadvantaged are made between the players.
- Next, angry exchanges give way to tense and complex negotiations. It's a cliffhanger. Will they make the deadline?
- Eventually, the budget deadline arrives and the crisis reaches full flower. The state is broke. The apocalypse is imminent: the poor will starve, civil servants will go without pay, and the government will grind to a halt. But somehow, this never happens. It's too bad. If government did shut down for a few weeks, if it actually stopped spending, the budget deficit would disappear on its own. Even better, people who pay taxes would discover how little we receive for those taxes—and how little we need government.
- But government goes on, paying bills with IOUs. The governor and legislature agree on a budget filled with "painful cuts." The politicians shake hands.
- Finally, because spending has been "cut to the bone," few notice the final budget is fatter than ever. Total expenditures increase, so the stage is set for yet another performance.

Say It Again: No New Spending!

When politicos talk about the "budget," ask about spending.

The budget is just the governmentʼs version of a Christmas wish list. It's always bigger than last year, and it's always presented as if it is beyond the control of any mortal. The politicians and bureaucrats are happy to say, "We budgeted $57 billion." They're afraid to say, "We're spending $57 billion."

When they talk about "cuts," ask what they're cutting—the budget or spending.

They can always cut the budget. They put in plenty of padding. They never cut spending. That would violate the greatest taboo.

When they clear their throats and try to change the subject, put it to them this way: "I don't care about the budget. Just tell me whether you're spending more or less than last year."

They never want to talk about spending. They're always spending more, and the more they spend, the more they tax. And they know that the more they tax, the more restless taxpayers become.

When they talk about government being faced with inflation and growing "caseloads," ask them: "How about me?"

The government budget makers don't like to admit that families, as well as government, must contend with their own growing problems. Families have more children, an unemployed father, or a sick grandparent. Families, unlike government, can't tax their way out of trouble.

When the crisis is over, when the politicians finish making all those "painful budget cuts," ask them: "How much is this going to cost me?"

Stop Being Part of the Problem

"Why should anyone care about government spending? "The government has plenty of money. Let them spend it," say most victims.

They're right. The government has plenty of money. The problem is, the money is really your money and my money. Every time government employees spend more money, they take more from all of us. They tax us directly with sales and income taxes. They tax us with little-noticed taxes like the 24.5 cents California tacks on to the price of each gallon of gasoline you buy.[8] They tax us in the alternate waves of inflation and recession caused by government spending and borrowing.

Government produces nothing. Its only revenue is the money it squeezes from people through taxes. Whenever it spends more money on some people, it takes money from others.

You Can Do Something About It

Consider privatizing everything, including roads, schools, and justice. Allow competition. There is no job government can do better than private enterprise. Bite your tongue before you say, "There ought to be a law." Don't ask for government favors or handouts. If you're unhappy with your child's school, figure out how to teach your children yourself. Your child will be a grandparent before California's public schools can be straightened out.

If you work for the government, quit. Get an honest job in the private sector. If you're a government worker, realize that your self-righteous sense of duty is bunk. Even prostitutes deserve more respect than government employees.

If you're on the dole, get off. Figure out how to make yourself useful. Stop being one of society's parasites.

If you're a reporter, realize that government is the largest criminal operation in the country. The politicos use your professional "objectivity" as a handle to turn you into a mouthpiece for propaganda. Those of you who believe there are two sides to every story should start reporting how government activities lead to poverty, crime, homelessness, and general despair. You and your editors have been manipulated by Fabians. Would you print a fashion story on the Emperor's New Clothes and call it "objective"?

Think about a modest reform suggested by the California Taxpayers Association. The association wants the state of California to abandon "current-services" budgeting. Now the state takes current spending, and adds on for population increases, inflation, and growing "caseloads" (including public school pupils, welfare families, state employees, prison inmates, and political appointees), to create next year's budget.

The taxpayers' association says the state should switch to "priority budgeting." Forget last year. Start from scratch, set priorities, then spend money on programs that work well and eliminate those that don't.

No one listened. Now the state-budget analyst predicts—based on a current-services approach—an $8.6-billion deficit by July 1, 1994.[9]

We all need to repeat the same slogan over and over, and whenever you hear about a new program, it's good to remind those you know: "No New Taxes! No New Government!"

All figures on our chart are total expenditures—general fund, special funds, and bond funds. The information for the first eight years on the chart (1983–84 through 1990–91) comes from the annual Governor's Budget. The last two years are from a *Wall Street Journal* article of September 8, 1992. *The Wall Street Journal* cites the California state director of finance for its figures.

Budget totals come in all shapes and sizes, depending on the motives and the purity of heart of the source. Often only the "general fund" totals are cited. Sometimes the general fund and special funds totals are used. Finally, as in this piece, the bond expenditures totals are used.

[1] *Cal-Tax News,* January 15, 1993. Governor Pete Wilson is cited as the source.

[2] *Governor's Budget,* January 1993.

[3] Ibid.

[4] Ibid.

[5] Ibid.

[6] *Sacramento Bee,* September 3, 1992, p. 1. This is the amount the state would have spent if it went along, as it habitually does, with all the "normal" increases in caseloads and other costs.

[7] State Board of Equalization, *1992 Annual Report* for 1991–92, for local expenditures of $25,908,964,000; *Governor's Budget,* 1992–93, for state expenditures of $57,411,000,000; Department of Finance, Population Research, for population as of July 1, 1992, of 31,300,000. The cost per person divides to $2,662. A family of four pays $10,648.

[8] Look at our gas pumps. Four separate taxes add up to 24.5 cents.

[9] Elizabeth Hill at the Legislative Analyst's Office, as quoted in *Sacramento Bee,* January 1, 1993.

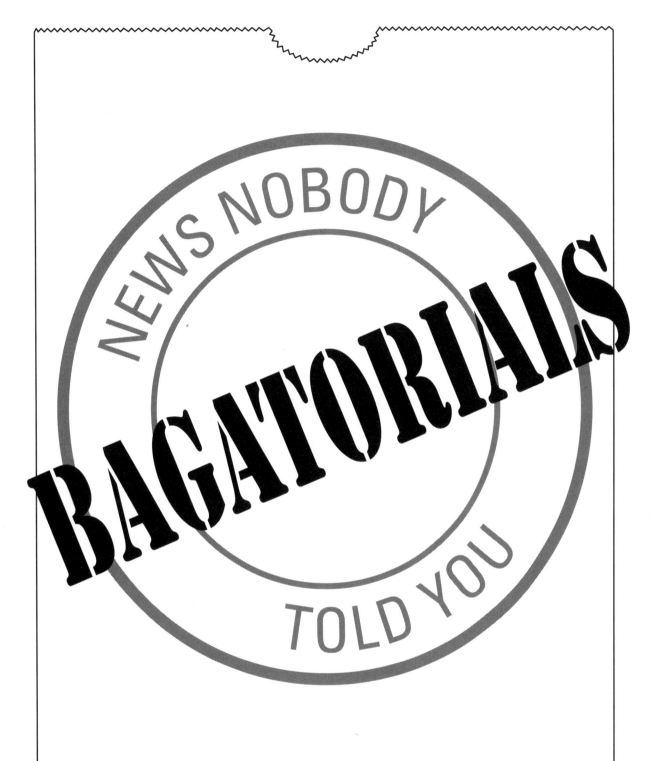

Use Water Freely

California has plenty of water. We use less than half the water that comes as rainfall. In addition, there are ample supplies of underground fresh water that can be tapped in times of less-than-average rainfall.

Unfortunately, the current system of state ownership of water has not supplied us and will not supply us with water where we need it when we need it.

We use the free-enterprise system to supply us with most of our needs. This system acts efficiently to match demand with supply. In the market system, people set prices for the goods and services we buy and sell. This price-setting forces us to prioritize our needs. We modify our needs and desires depending on our values and the prices we must pay for goods and services.

In California, the state owns the water. We can use it but we can't buy and sell it. Eastern European countries used a similar system for their entire economies. The Eastern European command economies were plagued with shortages, just like the Californian government-controlled water system. Eastern Europeans are trying to build a market system to distribute goods fairly, properly, and optimally. California must do the same for water.

THERE IS NO DROUGHT

Blue Canyon • *Major Sierra Watershed*

Year	Rainfall	Departure from Average	Average	% of Average	Yearly Averages
1984	79.52	16.85	62.67	126.89	
1985	49.36	-13.31	62.67	78.76	
1986	97.94	35.27	62.67	156.28	
1987	31.77	-30.9	62.67	50.69	
1988	45.75	-16.92	62.67	73.00	97.12%/5 yr.
1989	66.73	4.06	62.67	106.48	98.68%/6 yr.
1990	44.03	-18.64	62.67	70.26	94.62%/7 yr.

Sacramento

Year	Rainfall	Departure from Average	Average	% of Average	Yearly Averages
84/85	10.41	-6.69	17.10	60.88	
85/86	24.30	7.2	17.10	142.11	
86/87	11.69	-5.49	17.18	68.04	
87/88	12.96	-4.22	17.18	75.44	
88/89	13.04	-4.06	17.10	76.26	84.54%/5yr.
90/90	17.35	0.25	17.10	101.46	87.36%/6 yr.
90/91	11.78	-3.84	15.62	75.42	85.66%/7 yr.

Red Bluff

Year	Rainfall	Departure from Average	Average	% of Average	Yearly Averages
1984	34.04	1.52	21.51	107.07	
1985	17.04	-4.47	21.51	79.22	
1986	33.41	11.90	21.51	155.32	
1987	19.51	-2.00	21.51	90.70	
1988	19.85	-1.66	21.51	92.28	104.92%/5 yr.
1989	22.36	0.85	21.51	103.95	104.76%/6 yr.
1990	17.63	-3.88	21.51	81.96	101.50%/7 yr.

Fresno

Year	Rainfall	Departure from Average	Average	% of Average	Yearly Averages
84/85	7.94	-2.58	10.52	75.48	
85/86	14.83	4.31	10.52	140.97	
86/87	9.32	-1.26	10.58	88.09	
87/88	8.07	-2.51	10.58	76.28	
88/89	8.73	-1.79	10.52	82.98	92.76%/5 yr.
90/90	9.45	-1.07	10.52	89.83	92.27%/6 yr.
90/91	9.72	0.49	9.23	105..31	94.13%/7 yr.

THERE IS NO DROUGHT

Type of Water Use	No. of People	% of Water Used	% of Economic product
Residential, Municipal, and Industry	30,000,000	6%	97%
Agriculture	80,000	31%	3%
River Flows, Wildlife Preserves	0	63%	?
Totals	30,080,000	100%	100%

Many people recognize the need to do this. Farmers have large investments in land dependent upon water for their value. Homeowners have invested in landscaping. New residents require homes with adequate water.

Just as Poland and Czechoslovakia don't know how to dismantle and divide their state-owned economies, many Californians don't know how to divide up the water. Our position is that the initial allocation of rights is a small matter compared with the benefits of a market system. We can divide water rights evenly among all of us, or we can give rights based on past use. The best solution would be to give water rights to those who are using the water right now. This means giving the majority of water rights to farmers and farm interests.

As long as people are then free to buy and sell water, it doesn't matter who owns it initially. We could give watershed-ownership rights to a bunch of Martians. As long as they believed in capitalistic acts between consenting adults, we'd be in a better position than we are today. A clearing price for water would quickly establish itself. We'd soon have plenty of water at prices far below what most of us now think possible.

A lot of effort has gone into convincing you that there has been a drought. Cleanse yourself of that idea. California rainfall varies drastically from year to year. Over the past five years, we have averaged about 85 percent of the long-term rainfall average. The streamflow has been about sixty million acre feet instead of the long-term average of seventy-one million acre feet. Residents use less than 9 percent of the average streamflow. California has plenty of water. It has had plenty of water for the past five years.

The total residential water usage in California is so low in relation to supply that you are foolish to try to restrict your use. Your efforts will have an imperceptible effect. Even substantial actions of all residential and urban use combined will only have a small effect on the total amount of water used. Certainly you shouldn't waste any resource. On the other hand, don't let the watercrats dupe you into feeling guilty about the normal use of water.

Watercrats want you to feel guilty about using water. They use the old line Chinese Communist trick of publicizing the good peo-

THERE IS NO DROUGHT

Average California Water Supply and Usage

	Acre Feet
• Average Annual Streamflow	71,000,000
• Average Annual Underground Water Pumped	16,600,000
• **Average Total Water Available**	**87,600,000**
• Average Water Used by All Residential and Industrial Users	5,500,000
• % of water used by 30 Million residents and all industrial users	6.27%

ple who sacrifice for the state. They penalize those who use more than an arbitrarily deter-mined amount. If there is blame to lay in the California water situation, it is with the state-controlled system and the water bureaucrats who try to control our lives as puppets in their water follies.

Some people even want to put fish before people. The needs of man must come before the needs of fish. California can be a great place to live and work, so we are going to have growth, both from immigration and from our children. The only way to stop it is mass sui-cide, genocide, or sterilization. We should accept growth and plan for it rather than thinking we can stop it. We urgently need a market system for water. We need it at once. A free mar-ket is the only system that will work. Don't worry much about how to get to the free mar-ket. Just worry that we get there.

This bag is based on a number of articles and editorials.

California Water: Looking to the Future. Published in 1987 by the State of California Department of Water Resources. One of the best compendiums of official facts and figures. Copies are available at $5.00 each (plus sales tax) from the Department at P.O. Box 942836, Sacramento, CA 94236-0001.

If you write to us, we'll send you copies of these articles:

The Wall Street Journal . . . probably California's best source of news (editorial page, Feb-ruary 27, 1991).

The Economist . . . a weekly newspaper-magazine published in England, with journalistic standards far higher than American newsmagazines (February 16, 1991, pp. 16 and 25).

The Federal Reserve Board of San Francisco Weekly Letter ("Droughts and Water Markets" by Ronald Schmidt, March 15, 1991).

Barron's, November 26, 1990, p. 18.

Average annual streamflow in California is seventy-one million acre feet. There are wide variations in runoff. In 1923–24, it was 18.3 million acre feet. In 1937–38, it was 135 million acre feet. Present storage systems could capture forty-three million acre feet of this run off if they were all empty.

There are about four hundred large aquifers under California. They hold up to 850 million acre feet of fresh water. On average they supply 16.6 million acre feet of the water used in California.

The average family of five uses about an acre foot of water a year. An acre foot covers one acre of land one foot deep. Residents and industry use about 5.5 million acre feet a year.

Residents and industry can't cut usage enough to make a difference. This is only 6 percent of the total water available in an average year.

W ater seems cheap. Actually, the price varies a lot. The cost of water depends on the handling. Dams, pipes, and filtration cost millions. No one really knows what water's worth, because the market is so restricted.

To Farmers from the Central Water Project	$8*
To Homeowners, East Bay Municipal Water District	$397*
Desalinated in Santa Barbara	$1,900*

*Price per acre foot. An acre foot is 325,900 gallons.

Water rights are not like rights to most commodities. According to state water law, the state owns the water: water rights simply give people the right to use water, not to sell it.

Each acre of rice uses about three acre feet of water a year. There are between two and five hundred thousand acres in California planted in rice.

It Grows on Trees

Timber Is a Crop!

Some things you may not know about forestry

▼

Timber is a crop. The crop is grown on timberland. The harvest is houses, furniture, books, magazines, newspapers, cardboard boxes, computer paper, firewood, grocery bags, and the thousands of consumer products made from wood and wood derivatives.

There are plenty of trees. Since 1940, forest growth rates have exceeded harvest rates. According to Douglas Mac-Cleery of the U.S. Department of Agriculture's Forest Service, "By 1986, the volume of tree growth nationally exceeded the volume harvested by 37 per cent: and growth was 3½ times what it had been in 1920."[1]

There is plenty of timberland in the United States. There are 730 million acres of forest. That's about two-thirds the size it was in 1620, when the Pilgrims landed and the conversion to agriculture began. "Today, we have about the same area of both forests and cropland as we had in 1920.... Today, private forests comprise 73% of U.S. productive forest land, yet supply 80% of the wood volume harvested."[2]

"Foresters estimate that America's forest lands contain some 230 billion trees. More than 300 trees per acre. Using these figures, we can estimate that there are approximately 22 billion trees on forest industry land, 104 billion trees on nonindustrial private forest land, and 104 billion trees on public land."[3]

"Approximately 16 billion cubic feet (80 billion board feet) of timber is harvested within the United States each year. Some 20% of this is harvested on public land—13% on the national forests. Nonindustrial private forest provides 49.5% of the harvest, while forest industry lands provide 30.5%."[4] In 1990, we exported $6.5 billion in wood products and imported $5.2 billion in wood products.

"The United States has also worked to maintain its old growth heritage. The United States has 13.2 million acres of old growth trees—trees 200 or more years old. And over half that acreage, some 8 million acres, is protected within national parks, wilderness areas, and other administrative or legislative set asides."[5]

If You Love the Forest, Cut Timber Freely

All of the wood-products requirements for the United States and its exports could be grown on private land.

Timberlands are better managed by private interests than by public agencies. It cost $4 billion to run the United States Forest Service in 1994. Though the Forest Service has the oldest and the best trees in the United States, they manage the forest expensively, and poorly.

Private foresters know a lot about growing trees. They know a lot about how to cut and how to reforest areas that have been cut. Private foresters and timberland owners have been primarily responsible for the remarkable growth in our forests since 1900.

"I own my land and I own my trees. Let me be free!"

Clear-cutting makes sense. It costs less and increases yield for the timber owner, and it minimizes damage to land. Some of the most productive species, such as Douglas fir, must be clear-cut to insure future growth. Less land needs to be cut and fewer roads need to be built if clear-cutting is done.

Trees grow rapidly. With good forest practices, an entire forest can be cut and reforested every forty years.

It is more productive for society to grow trees to obtain wood products than to recycle. Recycling uses more resources than farming trees. Recycling costs time and energy. It also gives the government another opportunity to manage your life. That's why recycled products cost more. There is also a practical limit to recycling. With each recycling, the quality of the product decreases.

Privatize Timber

1. Many sections of the United States are ideal for growing trees. Let private-property owners grow and harvest trees on their land. Guarantee them the right to cut their trees when they want to do so. Make it a fundamental property right.

2. The United States Forest Service, which owns 191 million acres of timberland, must stop selling trees.

3. Decide how much of the 191 million acres of timberland should be kept as virgin forest. Give the rest to American citizens—just as the Czech Republic gave the state businesses to the entire population after the fall of communism. Let citizens sell their shares if they so choose—to those who will run parks or to those who will grow timber.

4. Timber-crop lands should be managed for the benefit of their owners. Put man's interests ahead of insects, fish, birds, and animals.

   Any society which does not put women and children ahead of men does not have a future. Any society which does not make human interests paramount above all others does not have a future.

5. If you want more trees, plant them. If you feel guilty about cutting down trees, plant a lot of them. Trees grow very easily. You can grow a lot of big trees in your lifetime. In the Pacific Northwest, people grow valuable Douglas firs in their backyards. A full-grown Douglas fir is worth about $1,000!

   We have so many trees growing now that it may not be economical, but you will feel better. Spend your time and your resources planting trees rather than complaining about what others are doing with the trees they own. Unfortunately, most of those who complain about trees being cut won't plant their own.

6. There are a lot of good causes in the world. One great cause would be to pick up all of the litter. Since most people live in urban areas, this would have a greater visual impact on most of us than the temporary visual losses from cutting and reforesting forest lands. Another great cause—which only you can accomplish—is to improve your own appearance.

7. You live in a world with economic realities. When it's economically feasible to have more trees, there will be more trees. People do things because it is beneficial to them. Recycling makes tree growing less productive.

8. If you think most timberlands aren't being used productively, get a window seat and fly from San Francisco to Seattle. Everything is forested, and everything is growing. If you wish to argue about these issues, learn the facts and use them honestly.

9. Do as you wish on your own land. If you want to buy virgin forestland and preserve it, do it. If you want to donate your funds to organizations that buy land and preserve it, do it, but don't expect to get what you pay for unless the organization faces a market discipline. Those who donate land to the government for preservation are the most foolish. Just as hunters do the most to protect wildlife, foresters do the most to protect trees.

10. The scientific management of forestland increases yields. Available evidence is conclusive: private forestlands are well managed. Obtain the facts and statistics for yourself. Review original material rather than just listen to the doomsayers who use misinformation and myths to form public opinion on this subject.

11. Paying tax dollars to anyone to grow anything is stupid. It hurts the honest timber growers who work without handouts. It wastes tax dollars. Public funds have been used for years to mismanage forestlands.

12. The Forest Service owns a lot of timber. This timber overhang affects the market price for wood products. Removing the Forest Service timber overhang from the market will temporarily increase the price of wood products. It will encourage tree planting and increase the supply of wood from private lands. In the long run, it will stabilize the industry and work to the benefit of both producers and consumers. If you pay more for wood products and much less for the taxes now wasted on bureaucracy, favors, compliance, and politics, you'll be richer.

Sound Knowledge from Tiny Facts Grows

- 16.5 billion cubic feet of wood are cut in the U.S. every year.
- 22.5 billion cubic feet of wood grow every year—37 percent more than used.
- The West Coast states produce 30 percent of the nation's lumber.
- Ten to fifteen billion board feet of lumber are imported each year. Most of it comes from Canada.
- "In the early 1900s, approximately 20 to 50 million acres were consumed by wildfires each year. Today, wildfire losses have been reduced to 2 to 5 million acres annually. . . ."[6]

Overgrown: The United States Forest Service

- It has an annual budget of $4 billion.
- It employs 31,536 permanent and accepted employees (1994).
- It controls eighty-five million acres of timberland and a trillion board feet of lumber.
- It spends $2.6 billion more than it takes in every year.
- It is forbidden by Congress from exporting timber.
- It sells much of its timber at 10–20 percent less than open market rates.

Defining Trees

Old growth: what those who don't want trees cut down call ancient forests. Generally it's one to two hundred years old.

Second growth: Trees that grow or are planted after old growth is harvested, or burned. Usually less than a hundred years old.

Become a Citizen Forester

If you are interested in planting trees, get a copy of *A Citizen Forester's Guide: The Simple Act of Planting a Tree, Healing Your Neighborhood, Your City, and Your World,* by Tree People, Andy and Katie Lipkis, published by Jeremy P. Tarcher, Inc., 5858 Wilshire Boulevard, Suite 200, Los Angeles, CA 90036

Good thoughts about trees are worthless without action. If you like trees, plant them. Trees can be ordered from: The National Arbor Day Foundation, 100 Arbor Avenue, Nebraska City, NE 68410, or call (402) 474-5655.

There are many statistics available on forests and the forest industry. Most of the figures have been compiled by the USDA/Forest Service, the Bureau of the Census, and other governmental agencies.

"The best time to plant a tree was twenty years ago. The second-best time is now."

—Anonymous

Trees

I think that I shall never see
a poem lovely as a tree

A tree whose hungry mouth is prest
Against the earth's sweet flowing breast;

A tree that looks at God all day,
And lifts her leafy arms to pray,

A tree that may in Summer wear
A nest of robins in her hair,

Upon whose bosom snow has lain;
Who intimately lives with rain.

Poems are made by fools like me,
But only God can make a tree.

—Joyce Kilmer

[1]Douglas MacCleery, USDA/Forest Service, *What on Earth Have We Done to Our Forests?,* USDA/Forest Service, Public Affairs Dept., P.O. Box 96090, Washington, D.C. 20090-6090, (202) 720-USDA.
[2]Ibid.
[3]American Forest and Paper Association, 1111 19th Street, N.W., Washington, D.C. 20036
[4]Ibid.
[5]Ibid
[6]American Forest and Paper Association, "Facts and Figures," p. 5.

The Air Is Cleaner

Air quality is better now than it has been for fifty years. Unfortunately, the air-quality tyrants choke us worse than ever. There is good news and bad news. Northern California has less air pollution now than at any time for the last half-century. The state Air Resources Board says:

> The Bay Area exceeded the federal ozone standard on only two days in 1990. It exceeded the state ozone standard, which is 75 percent of the federal standard, on fourteen days.

> The Bay Area exceeded the federal carbon-monoxide standard on only two days. The state carbon-monoxide standard, which is 10 percent lower than the federal standard, was exceeded on only five days in 1990.

Contrary to what most of us have been led to believe, air quality gets better and better. Automobile emissions are significant, but they accounted for only 31 percent of the total smog emissions in 1987.

Rainfall improves air quality. If we were in a normal rainfall period, we might not have exceeded the present standards on any day in 1990. Air quality is probably better than the figures indicate. James Sandberg, who works in the meteorology-and-data-analysis section of Bay Area Air Quality Management District (BAAQMD), told us that the amounts of rainfall in November, December, and January have an effect on the amount of particles in the air. The more rain during those three months, the fewer the particles and the lower the annual particulate average. Mike Basso, another BAAQMD employee, told us that when the public see haze, they become alarmed. He said haze is mostly water vapor that evaporates.

This is a big secret. Newspapers

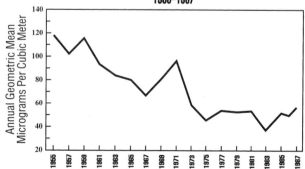

Total Suspended Particulate Levels (TSP)
1955–1987

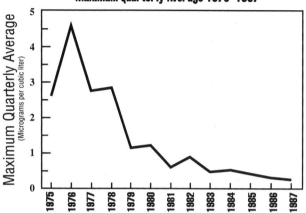

Particulate Lead Concentration, San Francisco Bay Area
Maximum Quarterly Average 1975–1987

such as the *San Francisco Examiner* advocate stiffer fines for air-pollution violations. Air-quality agencies contemplate bans and controls on charcoal briquets, gasoline-powered lawn mowers, leaf blowers, hedge trimmers, snow blowers, and chain saws. On December 21, 1990, U.S. District Court Judge Thelton Henderson "barred any future expansion of Bay Area freeways—including the construction of three big projects already approved—until transportation officials do a better job of analyzing traffic and smog," reported the *San Francisco Chronicle* on December 22, 1990.

The worst offenders are the air-quality and traffic dictocrats. "Air pollution kills people and [most] air pollution comes from automobiles," said Metropolitan Transportation Committee Chairman Rod Diridon of Santa Clara County (*San Francisco Chronicle,* June 28, 1990). Fear is their stock in trade: "We are rapidly approaching a danger zone. One day, we'll have to use gas masks to go outside," said Osby Davis, chairman of the Bay Area Air Quality Management Board (*Benicia Herald,* August 8, 1990).

"The last thing an environmental activist wants," writes Harry Browne, the noted investment adviser, in his *Harry Browne's Special Reports,* "is a solution to his problem—unless the solution is more government and more opportunities to force people to turn their lives upside down. . . . Almost all pollution is on government property—roads, rivers, oceans, lakes, air, and so forth. My home is clean, and I'll bet yours is too. It's the most natural thing in the world that owners of private property care more about the resources they use than people who camp in national parks, or who lease government timberlands or oil sites."

Power over you is the real issue

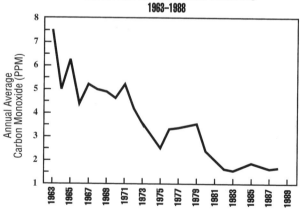

CARBON MONOXIDE LEVELS
1963–1988

Graph 2: Particulate Lead Concentration: shows the maximum quarterly average of lead concentration reported as micrograms found per cubic meter.

here, not air quality. Once one set of standards is reached, they lower the standards rather than give up their power. For years, the state standard for total suspended particulates (TSP) was one hundred micrograms per cubic meter for a twenty-four-hour period. In 1987, this measure was replaced with particulate measurement ten microns or less in size (PM-10) standard of fifty micrograms per cubic meter. The new measure is harder to achieve.

Most of this power involves money. The Metropolitan Transportation Commission has approved a plan that calls for raising the one-

> # **D**efinitions:
>
> Draconian: 1: of, relating to, or characteristic of Draco or the severe code of laws held to have been framed by him 2: extremely harsh or cruel: RIGOROUS.
>
> Statist: n: an advocate of concentration of economic controls and planning in the hands of a highly centralized government.
>
> Tyranny: 2: oppressive power; specif: oppressive power exerted by government.

dollar toll on state-owned bridges to two dollars. The plan calls for a combined gasoline tax and smog fee that could result in gasoline that costs four dollars per gallon. They've proposed that employers charge workers a seventy-five-dollar- per-month parking fee and pay for the conversion of vehicles to more expensive, "cleaner" fuels (*San Francisco Chronicle,* June 28, 1990). The overall cost of the plan has been estimated at $600 million per year in higher tolls, taxes, and fees (*San Francisco Chronicle,* November 29, 1990).

The bureaucrats, the statists, and the dictocrats plan to use this issue to reduce your freedom, no matter what the facts are. They seek to put the price of slavery into parts per million of pollution. There are simple and economical steps that can be taken to make dramatic reductions in automobile emissions without millions of tax dollars and an army of bureaucrats. We will present one of these solutions on our next bag.

Graph 4: BAAQMD Carbon-Monoxide Excesses: This graph shows the number of days the level of carbon-monoxide readings exceeded the eight-hour national standard.

If you would like further information on this issue, please write to us at: Clean Air & Freedom, P.O. Box 886, Benicia, CA 94510.

To confirm the statements on this bag, please call: Metropolitan Transportation Commission, Bay Area Air Quality Management District, State Air Resources Board, (916) 322-7074 (ask for Shelley Landino, air pollution specialist in the Technical Support Division).

You're the Victim of
A Legal Crime Called Redevelopment

Redevelopment threatens the homes, jobs, and futures of millions of Californians. Redevelopment laws allow officials to circumvent property rights so they can transfer land from regular people to the rich and powerful. Condemnations and evictions can come quickly in redevelopment. Compensation is minimal, especially after redevelopers use their tricks to force people out. Most renters and leaseholders receive nothing.

Bureaucrats love redevelopment's tax powers. Taxes are rerouted from normal uses to pay the redevelopment area's own bureaucracy. In effect, government steals from itself. Politicians thrive on the huge campaign contributions from the developers, who in turn profit from property lifted from owners. The developers build gigantic projects you know are a big waste of money, but with all the subsidies and guarantees offered by the bureaucrats, redevelopment is a no-risk proposition for a fat-cat developer. When the project goes belly up, the taxpayer is left holding the bag. Redevelopment is a legal crime and you're the victim.

It's a fascist process, run with fascist* tactics designed to benefit the rich, the powerful, and the bureaucrats. Redevelopers offer ideal communities to be filled with ideal people. Frankly, you won't fit in unless you're one of the chosen few. If you're in a redevelopment district, the district has an option to take your property. Your ignorance and your silence allow redevelopment to continue.

Redevelopment May Happen Here

You may already live or work in a redevelopment area. There are over 375 California redevelopment agencies to supervise 648 development projects. Cheaper! was surprised

---

*Fascism:"1. A philosophy or system of government that is marked by stringent social and economic control, a strong centralized government usually headed by a dictator.... 2. Oppressive or dictatorial control." From *The American Heritage Dictionary*, Second College Edition, 1976.

to find that fifty-five of our stores have been sucked into redevelopment areas. New areas are formed quietly, maybe even without your knowledge or approval. Sometimes an entire city will be turned into a redevelopment district.

How Does Redevelopment Work?

Redevelopment starts with somebody who wants something for nothing. Maybe it's a developer who wants subsidies, low-cost land, or a greased path through planning controls. Maybe it's a bureaucrat who wants to pull out a larger share of local taxes. Maybe it's a politician who figures redevelopment will lead to the big developers and their campaign donations. Or maybe it's a special interest that wants to settle a score with its neighbors.

First, your area will be declared "blighted." It will become hard to sell your land. Businesses become "nonconforming uses," so remodeling or selling the business is practically impossible. Your property values will go down. Eventually, you will be forced to sell to the government at their price. Redevelopment cancels property rights. The redevelopment district has an option to buy your property for the life of the redevelopment district. This may be for the next forty years or forever. It's a low price option. Under redevelopment, the government gets the benefits of any appreciation in the value of your property.

How Redevelopment Hurts You

Redevelopment may force you to move even if you want to stay put. You'll hear it's for the good of the district. Redevelopers don't care how long you've stayed in one place. Redevelopers don't care how well you've cared for the property.

Redevelopers don't care if you want to live out your life in familiar surroundings. Retirees are especially devastated by redevelopment. If you're in a redevelopment area, you can forget about leaving your property to your heirs.

It's likely redevelopment will bring you a strange new neighbor. Homes around you may be abandoned. Tramps will camp out next door. That new industrial park across the street may be loud, noxious, and subsidized by tax dollars. Your own use will probably become "nonconforming." You'll never get a permit to improve it. You're stuck until you decide to get out.

If you have a business in the district and redevelopers take the property, you will receive nothing for the value of your business. If you are a tenant, you will receive nothing. Redevelopers may pay for the cost of moving you to a new location, but they'll pay nothing if they force you out of business in the process.

Redevelopment creates public debt to build things that wouldn't be built if they had to compete in the market. Many of these projects land in bankruptcy, just like projects built in the S & L scandal. Redevelopment is promoted by people who have something to gain that can't be gotten in the free market.

Taxpayers pay the cost of attorneys in redevelopment. Some attorneys will be working on sneaky ways to grab land. Others will be defending suits brought by other government agencies that have lost tax dollars. "Let's you and me fight and we'll force the taxpayer to pay for it," say the lawyers to each other. Redevelopment increases the cost of government by adding another level of bureaucrats and another level of lawyers.

Redevelopment shows that government officials don't trust the American Way. Planners have a naïve and arrogant faith in the wisdom of the state. They see free markets as failures. They see their own Byzantine planning processes as constructive. They don't trust you to make the best decisions for yourself. They believe government knows best. It's ironic that the noble motives of planners so often make the world a worse place to live.

How Redevelopers Commit Their Crimes

Redevelopers are slick. They'll lie if it helps them to take your property, but they'll be very self-righteous about lying. They'll be outraged when you question their motives, even if they just received $25,000 from a developer. Their presentations will be beautiful, because the taxpayer will pay for the consultant's report. Redevelopers lack any sense of truth, honor, or justice. After all, most are politicians.

Redevelopers love secrecy. They will try to form the redevelopment district without arousing residents and property owners. There are legal requirements of notification, but redevelopers find slick ways to get around the restrictions. They make mistakes on addresses. They forget to mail notices. They add redevelopment on to agendas at the last minute. They hold meetings at strange times in strange places.

Redevelopment corrupts local planners and politicians. Stretch limousines show up to whisk local council members off to a night of high living at a fancy restaurant. "Just getting to know you," winks the developer. With hundreds of thousands of dollars at stake, redevelopment promotes bribery of officials. In redevelopment, government even steals from itself. Redevelopment law allows the redevelopment district to claim a larger share of taxes. Taxpayers pay the cost of the attorneys on both sides of the battle. Tax money that should have gone to pay for police, schools, and roads ends up paying redevelopment consultants.

Redevelopers are experienced. They know they know more about the process than you know. Assurances come easy to them. You'll hear blatant lies passed off as truth. You'll hear promises that can never be fulfilled. Different groups hear different answers, because redevelopers divide to conquer. Those who speak up will be silenced with slick meeting skills. A redeveloper believes the end justifies the means.

Redevelopers are patient. "Nothing will happen for several years. Don't worry," they'll assure you. Redevelopment districts are typically formed for thirty or forty years, but few redevelopment advocates can point to a completed redevelopment project. Once in redevelopment, planners and developers have a license to steal your property. Delay means they're still looking for the best way to turn your property to their advantage.

What Is a Redevelopment District?

Redevelopment is a legal form of coercion to take your property and business away from you in order to redistribute it to others. Those with the most money, political connections, and political clout will come out ahead. The rest lose.

The state passed redevelopment laws in the 1940s to spur renewal of urban areas that had fallen into neglect during World War II. After several revisions, cities and counties won the right to identify blighted areas and to cancel property rights in those areas. Once the agency is created, it can borrow against future tax revenues to fund the redevelopment plan. Redevelopment was started as "urban redevelopment" or "urban renewal." It's the same process that built the notorious, forbidding towers now called housing projects. In 1990, the federal government reported that more than a hundred thousand of the nation's 1.4 million public-housing units were uninhabitable.

After Proposition 13, California bureaucrats figured how to use this process for their own purposes. They still love to take over private property, to demolish homes and businesses, but they have lost interest in building homes for the poor. Now they're fascinated by something called "the downtown renaissance." Now, even if the bulldozer rips up farmland and turns it into a warehouse club, it's still "redevelopment."

Redevelopment has a record of failure. All together, the California Community Redevelopment Agencies owe about $20 billion. The projects pay interest of about $1 billion per year. Many of the projects, such as the major downtown hotel in Sacramento, are pretty shaky. So much is owed that local governments can't afford to shut down redevelopment agencies.

Why Cheaper! Cares About Redevelopment

Redevelopment is fascism. Redevelopers enjoy dictatorial powers over the property of others. The Redevelopment Board can reward favorites and punish transgressors. If you didn't object to the district before it was formed and you didn't file suit in sixty days after its formation, your legal rights are practically zilch.

We lost a store to redevelopment in 1991. In 1976, we built a store in Cordelia. Over a fifteen-year period, we operated a business by taking care of customers. In the mid-1980s we spent over $400,000 to improve the store and gasoline facilities. Several years later, the City Council of Fairfield, sitting as the Redevelopment Board, forced out over fifteen of our neighbors, including residents and businesses. After a fight, they paid us nothing for the business we built—just something for the real estate. Our neighborhood was cleared for a Price Club that received tax and development incentives to put a store at our location.

Redevelopment can be beat. In Pacheco, residents forced redevelopers to stop the redevelopment process. In West Sacramento, residents have thrown a monkey wrench into the redevelopment plans. In Half Moon Bay, local activists say, "Redevelopment fairy tales have lost credibility." They've forced the local press to report the truth about redevelopment. Today, Half Moon Bay officials spend less on consultants, less on studies, and less on other redevelopment boondoggles.

What If You Suspect Redevelopment Is Starting?

- *Act quickly! Start screaming!* Go door to door with petitions to block the formation of any new redevelopment district. Write a letter to the city, county, and local agency to object to the formation of a district! Start stirring things up. You're best off if you stop the district before it's formed. You don't need to pay a lawyer, but you do need to find someone who can talk to you about the legalities of redevelopment.
- *Suspect the worst!* Planners have told us they can always work around an outraged community. Planners will suggest a committee to study the area. They'll write a report on the use of redevelopment. The committee will be packed with dupes and toadies. Committee members will sit in judgment on your home. Instead, in almost every case, they'll choose the grand designs offered by planners and consultants. In those moments, they'll savor the sweet aroma of power. Those who resist will be labeled "Cynical" and cowed into silence.
- *Keep watching carefully!* If at first redevelopers don't succeed, they try, try again. Fabulous sums of money are at stake for those secret backers behind a redevelopment area. Those secret backers will watch patiently for the community to stop paying attention. They will "forget" to notify local residents of meetings. They will reschedule meetings without notice. In some areas, the local newspa-

per will be co-opted by the developer. You'll have to talk to your neighbors. You'll have to watch the official agenda every week.

- *Rely on yourself!* Whole neighborhoods are wiped out by redevelopment because every neighbor expects all of the other neighbors to speak up. Some of your neighbors may be deluded by the redeveloper's assurances. Others will be bought off. Some will be taken out of the redevelopment area in exchange for silence. If you want to save your property, you must speak for yourself.
- *Be unreasonable!* Typical redevelopers have been through the process many times. They know enough meeting tricks to keep you from talking and to keep the crowd from hearing the truth. Expect important people to ridicule you from the podium. Expect some of your neighbors to become toadies of the politicians. Resolve to complain to the politicians frequently and fervently. Understand you are dealing with cheats and thieves: redevelopers expect to steal your property rights in the name of the public good—or whatever else works. You'll hear about the good of the whole, as if individual initiative and individual prosperity were contrary to the public good.
- *Drum up support!* Find allies! Call the cities, counties, and taxing districts who will lose taxes when the redevelopment district is approved. Make up flyers and picket signs. Mail a couple of flyers to any out-of-town landowners who don't realize they will lose their land. Call the newspapers. Call the radio stations! Call the TV stations! Demand coverage! Find people who are going to lose their homes, their businesses, their employers, and tell them about redevelopment.
- *Find fault* with the redevelopment plan! Redevelopers must prove your area is blighted. They'll say your property is defective in design or construction, obsolete or overcrowded or just "socially and economically maladjusted." Prove you're doing well with your own property. Put yourself in the best possible position to sue the redevelopers if they form the district despite your objections.
- *Decide how you'll respond* to temptation when they try to buy you off. The squeaking wheel gets the grease. If they can figure a way to keep you quiet, they'll do it. If you get a deal, get it in writing. Many are promised. Few receive.
- *Discover the identity* of the strongest advocate for redevelopment. Is it a developer? A politician? Redevelopment, say redevelopers, is for the common good. Antiredevelopment experts say that behind every redevelopment district there's a big money interest. Expose it.
- *Call us at 800-9-Cheaper!* We can't attend every fight, but we fight hard for one of our stores. We've lost a store to redevelopment, so we know the costs of inaction. You're best off if a district is never formed. Once it is formed, you must work even harder to protect yourself.

What If You're Already in a Redevelopment District?

- *Realize* you don't have a future in this location. You don't have the property rights you thought you had. The redevelopment district has an option to buy your property, case closed. Your future has already been stolen.
- *Watch the Redevelopment Agency* and its progress. Find out who is prospering. Publicize the crooked deals. Find out who is giving favors to whom. Who is paying for those limousines public officials take to the luxury restaurants? Who received a new Jeep Cherokee as a gift from longtime supporters?
- *Block the redevelopers.* Try to find legal objections to their schemes. Band together with others to file suits against the district and its administrators. Make their lives difficult. Make them want to restore your property's legal standing outside of redevelopment. This is your only method of receiving market value for your property. We were the last to leave in Fairfield, and we received another location in return, thanks to thousands of customers and neighbors.
- *Find a new location.* Check it carefully. Ask the realtor about redevelopment before you buy in your new location. Next time, be more careful.

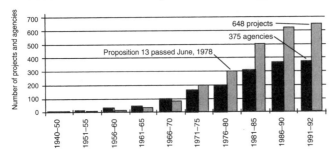

More Redevelopment Every Year

If redevelopment doesn't outrage you, we're surprised. If you'd like additional information on redevelopment, or if you'd like to refute our arguments, write to us at: Preserve Property Rights, P.O. Box 886, Benicia, CA 94510. We'll send you a packet of material we've collected. Some of the state's most knowledgeable experts are in Half Moon Bay. They've collected horror stories from around the state because they're trying to save their homes and Half Moon Bay from disaster. We need to know more about redevelopment, so, if you know more, we'd like to hear from you. We want to protect our business and our livelihoods and what remains of our personal freedoms.

In Germany they came first for the Communists, and I didn't speak up because I wasn't a Communist. Then they came for the Jews, and I didn't speak up because I wasn't a Jew. Then they came for the trade unionists, and I didn't speak up because I wasn't a trade unionist. Then they came for the Catholics, and I didn't speak up because I was a Protestant. Then they came for me, and by that time no one was left to speak up.

— *Martin Niemoeller*

Consider Smoking

**Smokers deserve the same respect as anyone else.
They make rational decisions. Consider for yourself.**

Life is terminal. Smoking won't affect the certainty of your mortality. Avoiding cigarettes will not ensure eternal life. You should smoke if it makes your life better.

Smoking may help you more than it hurts you. Smoke affects different people in different ways. Some people suffer immediate and severe reactions to cigarettes. Some people smoke for years without affecting their health. If smoking doesn't kill you, something else will.

Abstinence is not virtue. You won't go to hell for smoking. You won't go to heaven for just saying "No." Smoking isn't a moral decision.

Smokers know the cost of smoking. More Americans can recite the alleged effects of smoking than know the name of the President of the United States. Smokers also pay more than the cost of smoking. If smoking causes illness and shortens life, society spends less on smokers who die early than it spends on nonsmokers. If you die sooner, you'll receive less in Social Security and pensions.

Smoking may please you. For some, it is a complement to companionship. For others, it is a small self-indulgence. For a few, smoking is one of the most enjoyable experiences in their lives. Those who never smoked never learned the benefits of smoking.

You own your own body. It's your most valuable property. You are never broke as long as you live, and you can decide how to apply yourself as long as you do not damage others. If you wish to destroy yourself, it's up to you!

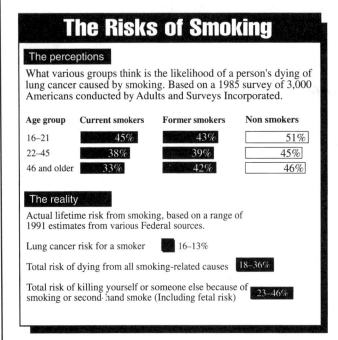

The Risks of Smoking

The perceptions

What various groups think is the likelihood of a person's dying of lung cancer caused by smoking. Based on a 1985 survey of 3,000 Americans conducted by Adults and Surveys Incorporated.

Age group	Current smokers	Former smokers	Non smokers
16–21	45%	43%	51%
22–45	38%	39%	45%
46 and older	33%	42%	46%

The reality

Actual lifetime risk from smoking, based on a range of 1991 estimates from various Federal sources.

Lung cancer risk for a smoker — 16–13%

Total risk of dying from all smoking-related causes — 18–36%

Total risk of killing yourself or someone else because of smoking or second-hand smoke (Including fetal risk) — 23–46%

To quit is costly. When you quit, you may suffer from "tension, restlessness, irritability, increased hunger, inability to concentrate, light-headedness, and insomnia," according to Dr. Siegel in his book *Intoxication*. Those who smoke may become more creative and decisive after a cigarette. They may be more mellow than non-smokers. Nicotine stimulates and relaxes.

Many who quit smoking become jerks. The debate on smoking has been held between hyperventilating health fascists and self-righteous busybodies addicted to telling others what to do with their lives. Smokers should decide for themselves. The most vociferous anti-smoking activists are former smokers, anxious to recover their own misspent youth out of the lives of others. Who could wish to become so twisted?

You can smoke *and* be considerate of others. The epidemic of secondhand smoke symptoms, including nausea, pallor, weakness, headache, dizziness, abdominal pain, and an uncontrollable urge to make loud and obnoxious complaints rather than saying "Excuse me, would you mind not smoking here?," are mostly inconsiderate hypochondriac behaviors by non-smokers. Smokers, on the other hand, have become quite gracious as they huddle in corners and doorways.

It's relatively easy to quit smoking. Just stop putting the cigarettes in your mouth. You already know many people who have quit smoking. If you want to quit, there are dozens of good ways to change your behavior, including prescriptions, hypnosis, classes, and a host of home remedies.

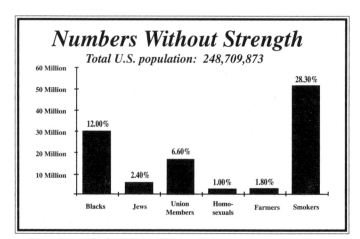

Numbers Without Strength

Total U.S. population: 248,709,873

Blacks	12.00%
Jews	2.40%
Union Members	6.60%
Homo-sexuals	1.00%
Farmers	1.80%
Smokers	28.30%

Source: Bureau of Labor Statistics, 1991, from 1990 census

To smoke is to demonstrate one's personal liberty. Even if smoking is made illegal, people will smoke. No matter how much school time is wasted on the horrors of smoking, people will choose to smoke. The politically correct antismoking message is too pat for independent thinkers. They will smoke to judge the truth.

There's already more than enough jealous surveillance of your personal habits than there ought to be in a free society. If you don't smoke, mind your own business. If you want to smoke—enjoy! If you choose to abstain—be happy!

Government at all levels taxes and abuses smokers in every way imaginable. Despite their numbers, smokers have neither rights nor champions. Consider how smokers stack up against other categories.

Why are smokers fair game for tax and abuse while other minorities enjoy special consideration and advantages? Because Americans can be abused in the way they spend their money.

WARNING: 51,605,900 adult Americans smoke. That's 7,877,525 more people smoking than voted for Clinton in the 1992 presidential election. Over 28.3 percent of all Americans over eighteen years old smoke. Smokers are America's largest and most despised minority.

Smokers Pay Their Own Way

For purposes of argument, assume that medical research has proven a direct causal link between smoking and disease. Even then, it does not follow that society incurs costs because of tobacco consumption. One analyst reported:

A 1989 study by the Rand Corporation found that the state and federal excise taxes on cigarettes—which, together with sales taxes, represent 25 to 55 percent of the retail price—are sufficient to cover the net costs of smoking. The researchers noted that smokers tend to die early, thereby reducing the need for nursing home care and demands on Social Security and pension funds.

Tobacco users already more than pay their way through taxes; therefore the cost to the taxpayers of reducing tobacco use will actually exceed the benefit to society.

—Bennett and DiLorenzo, *Official Lies: How Washington Misleads Us.*
Please check out the reading list at the end of this essay.

Tobacco Money Doesn't Buy Protection

Buying politicians is cheaper than most people believe. During the eighteen-month period from January 1, 1991, to June 30, 1992, tobacco political-action committees gave

$578,390 to U.S. senators. Members of the U.S. House of Representatives received $1,161,474 from tobacco interests. Of course, tobacco companies gave money to almost every other elected official in the country, including Willie Brown. The Speaker accepted $221,332 during the 1991-92 election period.

This was money poorly spent. An honest politician is one who stays bought, but the recipients of tobacco money continued to pass discriminatory taxes and restrictions on smokers faster than ever before. Political action is a waste of money for both tobacco companies and smokers. Our source is *Public Citizen*'s report on "Tobacco Money, Tobacco People, Tobacco Policies" (October 26, 1992, by Andrew Carroll).

More than 63 percent of the purchase price of our USA cigarettes is tax ($9.89 per carton, plus sales tax, equals $10.68; inside the $9.89 is $5.90 in direct taxes). "Once discriminatory taxes are assessed against a despised minority, it is only a matter of time before they become oppressive. . . . Taxation without some concrete form of restraint knows no limit," writes Charles Adams in his book *For Good & Evil*.

Do you worry about taxes wasted on newspaper, radio, and billboard space to crusade against tobacco? Probably not—but when government bribes the media to campaign against the evils of smoking, you ought to wonder if the end justifies the means. When a traditional bulwark of personal liberty has been paid to advocate the growth of government, our freedom is diminished. Freedom or health? To force us to choose is insidious.

This pattern was set by the California Lottery. Now the state promises the media large sums of money to be spent advertising something if it is approved by the legislature. The press then falls over itself in praise for the state's proposed action. Example: The State Lottery Commission is exempt from Truth in Advertising laws. Last year, the state paid the media $41,128,811 to promote gambling in California. Crooked media are just as bad as crooked politics.

Our sources are the California State Lottery Fund Financial Statement, June 30, 1992, and the Cigarette and Tobacco Surtax Fund.

Why We Sell Cigarettes

We make our living serving customers. Our customers want cigarettes. We supply cigarettes better than other stores. If you smoke, please consider buying cigarettes from Cheaper! because:

- Our everyday low price of 99 cents on a pack of USA cigarettes is the best price on the market for an all-tobacco, additive-free cigarette. If you prefer an advertised brand, consider a pack of Marlboro for only $1.99 plus tax.
- Our everyday carton prices start at $9.89 on USA (which is our best cigarette

and our lowest-priced). We are Cheaper! for cartons of advertised brands such as Winston or Kool. If you prefer a Philip Morris blend (which has better than a 50-percent share of market in this area), we sell F&L, Gridlock, and Money Menthol, which are made by Philip Morris, Cheaper!

- We stock over three hundred brand styles of cigarettes. Every style is in stock every day. If we run out of stock, we send you a gift certificate for five dollars. We search out and participate in every coupon and manufacturer promotion available, so you can always buy the best deal.
- We sell grocery staples, such as milk, bread, beans, rice, pasta, beer, soda, diapers, and other groceries, at everyday Cheaper! prices.

Cigarettes are a very big business. Americans smoke over five hundred billion cigarettes each year. That's 2.5 billion cartons, or twenty-five billion packs of cigarettes. While smoking has declined, despite all the negative publicity, total usage has declined by less than 1.6 percent per year in ten years.

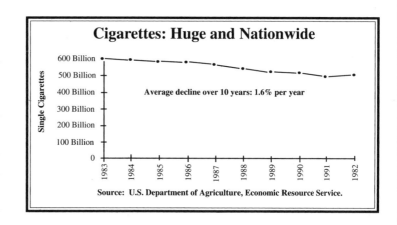

Cigarettes: Huge and Nationwide

Average decline over 10 years: 1.6% per year

Source: U.S. Department of Agriculture, Economic Resource Service.

Why You Should Stop Smoking

To smoke or not to smoke is an important decision. Actions have consequences. Here are our arguments against smoking:

1. You may decide it's bad for your health. Smoking may cause you to age ten to fifteen years faster than nonsmokers.
2. Your friends and family may urge you to stop.
3. It costs a minimum of $389 per year to smoke (at the rate of one pack per day).
4. Being hassled by nonsmokers is horrible.
5. You may decide you don't enjoy smoking.
6. You may decide you offend people by smoking. You are very sensitive to others.
7. You plan to live forever and you want to be healthy during your long and productive life.

8. Smoking stinks. Your clothes smell like smoke. So does your furniture. Your teeth are yellow. Your fingers are stained.
9. You're tired of being treated like a second-class citizen.

Reasons to Smoke

1. It's pleasurable. It adds to your enjoyment of life.
2. It's something you can afford to do. Besides, there are a lot of risks in life.
3. It relieves boredom.
4. Quitting is worse than continuing.
5. Your health is fine. You know you are mortal. You are skeptical of government studies. Government lies about most topics. Probably this one too.
6. You like the taste of tobacco.
7. It helps relieve stress. It helps you relax.
8. It helps you get your work done.
9. To paraphrase Winston Churchill: "You've taken more out of tobacco than tobacco has taken out of you."
10. You are ornery. Smoking shows people you are your own boss.

How We Oppose Smoking

We advocate the freedom to engage in capitalistic acts between consenting adults. For years, we've thought it in our best interests to get our work done without smoking. We've also helped many of our employees stop smoking.

Our office has been smoke-free since the company was started in 1964. We've paid $100 per month per store bonuses to the staff of stores that are completely nonsmoking. We've increased the salary of longtime employees by up to $1,000 per year when they quit smoking. Others were sent on luxury trips as a reward for giving up the habit. We've paid for the cost of hypnotists, smoke-ending programs, and patches for employees and their spouses who say they want to quit smoking.

We've talked at length about the health risks of smoking. From time to time, we've computed the annual cost of smoking and told employees the sum. Our nonsmoking employees pay $100 per month less for medical insurance than our smoking employees.

Employees who do not smoke tend to be healthier, get more work done, and are generally more effective than smokers. We believe our medical costs are lower for nonsmokers than smokers. We hire smokers, and we know it's up to an individual to choose to quit smoking. We try to help with some friendly persuasion.

Books We Recommend

James T. Bennett and Thomas J. DiLorenzo, *Official Lies: How Washington Misleads Us,* Groom Books, 18090 Diagonal Road, Alexandria, VA 22314 (quote on p. 228).

Charles Adams, *For Good & Evil: The Impact of Taxes on the Course of Civilization,* Madison Books, 4720 Boston Way, Lanham, MD 20706. We'll send you a gift certificate for five dollars if you read this book and tell us about it.

W. Kip Viscusi, *Smoking: Making the Risky Decision,* Oxford University Press, 200 Madison Avenue, New York, New York 10016. The "Roots of Smoking" chart itself draws upon more than one chart in the book—tables 4-2, 4-3, and 4-7, pp. 69, 70, and 77. To order the book, call 1-800-451-7556.

Ronald Siegel, Ph.D., *Intoxication,* 1989, Pocket Books, 1230 Avenue of the Americas, New York, NY 10020 (quote on p. 97).

False Charity vs. Real Charity

It's never enough and it does no good

In 1990, the National Marketing Service, a professional fund-raising company, coaxed $1 million out of Californians who wanted to help out the Children's Wish Fund. Those kind-hearted people were really helping out the National Marketing Service. The company kept 93 percent of the money!

The kids did fairly well by the standards of professional fund-raising. The Children's Wish Fund got 7 percent of the money raised by the National Marketing Service. That's ten times better than cancer victims who were the bait for the Walker Cancer Research Institute of Aberdeen, Maryland.

In a three-year period, the "research institute" raised more than $9 million and contributed $67,822—.7 percent—to cancer research. The rest of the money—$9,236,946—disappeared into the pockets of fund-raisers

Charities Sucked Dry

California Attorney General Dan Lungren thinks that's going too far. He says the Walker Institute is simply a "shell" used by fund-raisers and he's suing for fraud. As if that will eliminate greed! Even if Lungren wins the lawsuit, don't expect a court victory to change fund-raising.

Under the law, professional fund raisers can pull in huge amounts of money for charity and turn little, even nothing, over to charity. Furthermore, too few donors check to see what happens to their donations. They assume charity does good.

In 1990, the operators of nearly one hundred professional fund-raising campaigns in California forwarded less than 10 percent of their take to charity. Charities can even wind up owing money to their fund-raisers!

Nine charities got nothing, and one—California Abortion Rights Action League North—wound up owing Gordon & Schwenkmer, Inc., $163,542—even though the fund-raisers actually pulled in $334,280 in contributions.

Only one-third of all money raised for charity by professional fund-raisers in California goes to charity.

"After the telethon"

Many Questions, Few Scruples

The world of organized charity is full of questionable characters, but the professional fund-raisers are most despicable. They catch you off-guard by calling your home. They tug at your heartstrings by sending you envelopes with pictures of starving children.

The phone calls come at dinner or during the ninth inning of a tie ball game on television. The talk is smooth, the identity of the caller vague, but the cause is noble and they've caught you at just the right time: you're hungry or you're distracted by the ball game; you feel guilty because you're healthy; you're busy living your own life instead of joining the neighborhood crime watch; you've heard about battered children and you wish it would go away. So you say, "OK, put me down for twenty dollars." They do, and sometime in the next year or two, the fund-raisers send 60 cents to the poor.

That's exactly what the Pallottine Fathers of Baltimore pulled in a classic charity con of the 1970s. In a massive mail campaign, the religious order used photographs of "starving, sick and naked" children in the jungles of Brazil to prey on trusting, generous people. In one eighteen-month period, they raised $20 million. Three percent of the money went to the kids; the rest, $19.4 million, went to pay for mailings—and to finance high-flying real-estate deals and other pet projects of the chief fund-raiser, Father Guido Carcich.

After preying on trusting people for six years, Carcich got caught. He pleaded guilty to diverting money to his friends and family and was sentenced to eighteen months probation. The fund-raising operation was shut down.

Statistics Hide Condos and Concordes

So what should you do about it? Lungren suggests you check with the Better Business Bureau Philanthropic Advisory Service. The service publishes an Annual Charity Index.

Checking the index sounds like a good idea, but the statistics in the index actually cover up the charity industry's multitude of sins. Look up the index's 1991 listing for the United Way of America. It looks great: 90 percent of the United Way's income goes to worthy causes. Unfortunately, the truth is disgusting.

For more than a decade, William Aramony, former president of the United Way, was a rich man who traveled across the Atlantic on the high-speed, high-price Concorde and cruised through Washington and New York in limousines. Hotel rooms? Not good enough! Mr. Aramony stayed in condominiums. Aramony was a master of fund-raising. For his efforts he was paid over $463,000 a year in salary and benefits .

With an income like that, Aramony could afford to spend his own money on his first-class travel. He didn't. Money for limousine rides and supersonic flights came from working people across the country who contributed to the United Way campaign with their hard-earned dollars, through payroll deductions.

Aramony Sorry He Got Caught

Finally, someone noticed Aramony's luxurious life-style. After twenty-one years of fund-raising success and supersonic travels, Aramony quit—with a big pension, few regrets, and no apology. The uncrowned king of organized charity only regretted "any problems my lack of sensitivity to perceptions has caused the movement."

Aramony bent ethical standards into the shape of a pretzel but he broke no laws. One can lawfully get rich off of charity. The moral of this story? If you give to professional charity, you're a sap.

Bring Charity Back Home

Scrap the big impersonal and coercive charities run by layer upon layer of well-paid professionals! Bring back person-to-person charity. Begin with the people closest to us: our children and parents, or neighbors and co-workers, and the people we do business with. It's even better to give to panhandlers than to give to professional charity.

But who's going to help the millions of sick and homeless and unemployed, the helpless children without fathers, the bedridden old folks with no families?

How about their own families? With a few exceptions, their families are people who are alive and well but are indifferent. Most figured Social Security would take care of them. Big mistake.

Organized charities discourage individual acts of charity. In this system, people pay their taxes and contribute to charity, then retreat into a cozy dream world believing government and professional charities will take care of the problem.

Charity Industry Annual Salary and Benefits in America		
Ralph Dickerson	New York City United Way	$ 263,886
Betty Beene	Tri State United Ways·	260,067
Oral Suer	Washington DC United Way	231,165
Ben H. Love	Boy Scouts of America	231,100
Martin Kraar	Council of Jewish Federations	230,773
H. Clay Howell	Detroit United Way	215,805

Tri State United Ways is a federation of 35 United Ways in New York, New Jersey, and Connecticut. Source: **Chronicle of Philanthropy.**

In reality, organized private charities and public-welfare programs are remote, impersonal, bureaucratic, expensive, and, most important, ineffective.

Organized charities coerce with guilt. Their purpose is to get you to give, but you'll never know the results. "You can't refuse," they say, "to help these helpless people. Can you?" Of course you can—and you must.

Real Charity—Do what does good

- First, help yourself. Solve your own problems.
- Then, after you're squared away, help someone you know: your family, friends, fellow workers.
- Most of all, help those who have helped you.
- Give yourself, not just your money. Your time and sacrifice make the best gifts. Be effective. Help people face to face.
- Build up a goodwill bank. Try to keep yourself in a position not to require charity, but if you help others when they're in need, you can draw on that goodwill when you need it.
- Give because you want to give, not because you feel guilty or threatened. Real charity is voluntary. Remember, you're in control—not the beggar on the street with his precious cat, not the telethon host hugging a helpless child.
- Practice restraint. In your enthusiasm to do good, you might cause harm. The object of charity is not to make you feel good but to do good for someone else.
- Don't give money to people who want to help others but can't manage their own money.
- Never buy a ticket to a charity banquet. These gaudy affairs do more good for the publicity-hungry philanthropists than for the truly hungry.

- Save money for a rainy day—not just to survive your own hard times but to help others survive theirs.
- Beware of giving gifts that become part of someone's budget and need to be renewed endlessly.
- Thank others when they help you.
- You have no obligation to help others. That's one of the beauties of true charity.
- Take precautions. Get insurance. Work to avoid being a burden yourself. Oakland homeowners might have prevented fire damage by clearing brush. Most fire losses could have been insured ahead of time.
- Before you fly off the handle, angry about charity, think this through. Does it matter why you want to be charitable? Does it matter what you give as long as you use your own resources and not those you coerce from your employees? The central issue in charity may be "Do you do the best that can be done with what you give?" We suggest you will do the best in those activities you perform most carefully.

Something for Something

Look at the front of most of our stores and you'll see a sign advertising some of our good neighbors. We pay these neighbors—who include youth groups, Scouts, marching bands, churches, and community-spirited families—$100 per month in return for picking up the litter in the neighborhood around our stores. This is our basic "charity." Write us for a donation, and we'll send you an invitation to join in this something-for-something program. We charge everyone Cheaper! prices for merchandise, rather than giving it away to a few and charging more to everybody else. Our primary service is to provide Better! goods at Cheaper! prices. Reckless donation is contrary to the best interests of our customers and their community.

Don't let yourself be duped on

Food Irradiation!

by Petr Beckmann

Several tens of thousands of years ago, man conquered fire and subjugated it to his needs.

Do you know why this was such an epoch-making event? Not because of the heat in itself, or because of any space heating. The northern latitudes with their cruel winters were uninhabitable without fire. Before fire was tamed, man lived in Mesopotamia, Africa, China, Central America, and other tropical and semitropical places; what he did not need was more heat.

No, the taming of fire had a very different significance; it made man the only animal able to jump out of its original place in the food chain. Insects eat plants, and small birds eat insects, and birds of prey eat small birds. Man gathered berries, but only of a limited range. They had to be digestible, they had to be non-poisonous, they had to be soft enough to chew, void of thorns, and void of parasites, or he died before the wolves and bears ate him.

Fire changed all that. It softened inedible food, killed its parasites, and enormously widened the range of food available to man. (It also enabled him to move to regions previously prohibited by its severe winters.)

About ten thousand years ago, the second great food revolution took place: the agricultural revolution. No longer at the mercy of nature's charity, man learned to grow his own food and to husband his own animals.

But this food was subject to spoilage. To this day in the Third World, about one-third of

FOOD IRRADIATION:
THIS IS NOT WHAT
IT LOOKS LIKE.

MARCO POLO BEGAN TRADING FOOD-
PRESERVING SPICES, PAVING THE WAY
FOR THE SALT TALKS

the harvest falls victim to rodents, insects, rot, mold, and other forms of spoilage.

In advanced countries they learned how to preserve food—sort of. First they "salted it away," which made it—well, very salty. Even before the advent of refrigerators, people knew that food lasts longer in the cold, and they would break up the ice during the spring melt and transport it to caves, where it lasted through the summer. Electric refrigeration, when it came, was imperfect, took up space, and consumed much energy. To ship fruit and vegetables in refrigerated railroad trucks from California and Florida to the rest of the country was a triumph, but an imperfect one; tomatoes are shipped before they are quite ripe, left to "ripen" during the trip and at the store—but if you grow your own tomatoes to full ripeness, you know the difference. As for canning, I don't have to tell you that food out of a can is not the same as fresh food.

Chemical preservation has its drawbacks, too. Nitrates used in sausages, for example, are carcinogens—not terribly dangerous ones (for it is the dose that makes the poison), but still formally carcinogens. More important, chemical preservatives are ineffective against dangerous parasites such as the salmonella bacterium in chicken, the trichinella worm in pork, and several others.

Virtually all types of food spoilage—rot, mold, fermentation, etc.—are due to microorganisms. So is food poisoning, including the most common (70 percent), salmonellosis, and the most dreaded, botulism.

Some thirty years ago, a most wonderful way of killing these microbes without affecting the food was developed: irradiation. A strong dose of ionizing radiation (very similar to X-rays) will kill the microbes without significantly affecting the surroundings in which they live. At present, the most common application is not food irradiation but sterilization of disposable medical equipment—more than half of it, including devices permanently inserted in a patient's body, is sterilized this way.

EARLY CHEFS COOKED FOOD OVER AN OPEN FLAME.
THIS WOMAN'S DESCENDANT IS JULIA CHILD'S GREAT-GREAT-
GREAT-GREAT-GREAT-GRANDCHILD

The irradiated target cannot possibly become radioactive—at least not more than to begin with, for all foods and most other objects are slightly radioactive anyway. There is a very good physical reason why irradiation by gamma rays cannot induce radioactivity in the target. I will not bore you with that reason; instead, I will just ask whether you can imagine that physicians would allow devices to be inserted in bleeding wounds or other parts of the bodies of their patients if they were significantly radioactive.

LOUIS PASTEUR MADE GETTING A MILK MUSTACHE SAFER FOR EVERYONE!

What irradiation does to food is no less than wondrous. Irradiated strawberries will last for more than two weeks at thirty-eight degrees Fahrenheit without molding; pota- toes will not sprout for weeks even if not refrigerated; fruit like peaches and mangoes can be harvested after it has fully ripened, and only then is it shipped without danger of spoilage; and endless other applications. In general, the interval during which food stays unspoiled is prolonged from days to weeks, sometimes without refrigeration. Virtually all advanced countries have approved and are using food irradiation, though they approve and regulate each food group separately.

But, perhaps even more important, food irradiation protects you from disease. A signifi- cant fraction of raw chicken is infested with salmonella bacteria, and a significant fraction of raw pork is infested with microscopic trichinella worms (up to 30 percent in both cases, as random samples have shown). It is left to you to kill them by the high temperatures of fry- ing, roasting, etc., all the way through the meat.

What if you don't succeed? Here is the answer: thirty-three million Americans a year become ill due to microbial contamination of their food. Some four thousand (mainly very young and very old) die from severe salmonellosis. Trichinosis is a rare disease, and "only" some one hundred Americans die from it every year, though the number is rising, mainly because of the recent popularity of underdone "pink pork." But irradiated poultry and pork are salmonella-free and trichinella-free even when raw.

Unfortunately, the salmonella bacterium and the trichinella worm have powerful friends: organizations such as Food & Water, Inc., and other well-heeled groups who hate technology and want to deindustrialize America. They work with lies and, much worse, with half-truths, better denoted as three-quarter lies.

An example of an outright (and fantastic) lie is the

"The Department of Energy has a solution to the problem of radioactive waste. You're going to eat it," says a flyer from the anti-industry.

claim that the purpose of food irradiation is to let the nuclear industry get rid of its wastes. In fact, practically all irradiation is now performed by cobalt 60, which is specially made for the purpose in Canada, whence it is imported to U.S. irradiation plants.

Now for some half-truths, or, rather, three-quarter lies, by which the Luddites try to dupe you.

- They make the ominous claim that the radioactive doses to which foods are exposed are lethal. Darn right they are. So is the heat in a baker's oven lethal. What does that have to do with the wholesomeness of bread after it has been baked in it?
- They claim that chemical changes take place in foods during irradiation, and some of them might be dangerous. Yes, some very slight chemical changes do take place—in particular, a very small amount of so-called radiolytes appear in some foods. What they don't tell you is that these same radiolytes are present in nonirradiated foods, where they are produced by conventional processing such as cooking. Not a single substance absent from other foods has ever been detected in irradiated food.
- We cannot know, they direly warn, whether one day food irradiation will not reveal hidden hazards after all. But neither can we know this for frying, baking, canning, knitting, or playing bridge, for the simple reason that it is impossible to prove a negative.

However, food irradiation has been approved not only by the developed countries' special agencies and the World Health Organization, but by the world's most conservative and infuriatingly cautious health watcher, the U.S. Food and Drug Administration (FDA). It has only permitted the irradiation of poultry in 1992, though among the many tests was one, completed in 1985, in which six hundred thousand pounds of irradiated chicken meat was fed to several generations of test mice, hamsters, rats, rabbits, and dogs. The FDA is so overly—indeed, irresponsibly—careful that it literally lets Americans die for lack of drugs that have been approved for years in Europe but which the FDA is still testing. If the FDA has approved food irradiation (of wheat, flour, potatoes, fresh fruit and vegetables, spices, pork, and poultry, with further groups to be approved), I don't think you need be overly worried over this point.

Whom should you believe, me or the Food & Water Friends of Salmonella? Neither.

Truth is not found by choosing whom to parrot; it is found by comparing statements to all available facts. You cannot irradiate food yourself, but you can go to the library and read both sides of the issue and search for the holes that one side conceals and ignores. I am not worried that you will miss them; and you will have found the truth, not parroted its shadowy imitation.

(Try *Food Irradiation,* 1986, from Academic Press, New York; or send a letter to "Irradiated Truth," P.O. Box 886, Benicia, CA 94510, for a free copy of the authoritative Irradiated Foods from the American Council on Science and Health; or ask the librarian to help you.)

There is, however, one point that is more sinister than any physical, chemical, or medical considerations, and it is one that you can test yourself immediately.

All irradiated food in the U.S. is labeled as such by the "radura," an international symbol identifying it. As an American you can buy it if you want to, and you don't have to if you don't. It is not an election, where the majority decides for everybody, including the dissident minority, because there can be only one U.S. president and only one winning answer to a referendum. In contrast, buying irradiated food not only is your personal decision, but it does not affect anyone but you or your family.

Suppose the various Knights of Salmonella were right in all their dire warnings; why would they seek to influence a decision that does not affect them?

Because they are after political power. After political power of the kind that has drenched this century in blood, the coercive power that knows only two variants of activity: whatever is not forbidden is compulsory.

"Thou shalt eat what I eat" is the present battle cry of the superstition mongers; and more coercion, more uniformity, more totalitarianism will follow.

Don't let yourself be duped. Stand up for truth and reject the totalitarian superstition mongers. Protect the health of your children and your own freedom!

Petr Beckmann was professor emeritus of electrical engineering at the University of Colorado, Boulder.

Decide the facts and the law!

The Law in Your Hands

John Adams, second President of the United States of America, wrote: "It is not only {the trial juror's} right, but his duty to find the verdict according to his own best understanding, judgment and conscience, though in direct opposition to the direction of the court."

John Jay, the first U.S. Supreme Court chief justice, wrote: "The jury has the right to judge both the law as well as the fact in controversy" (*Georgia* v. *Brailsford,* 1794).

Thomas Jefferson told Thomas Paine in 1789 that "I consider trial by jury as the only anchor yet devised by man, by which a government can be held to the principles of its constitution."

Noah Webster, in his dictionary published in 1828, defines a jury as "a number of freeholders, selected in the manner prescribed by law, impaneled and sworn to inquire into and try any matter of fact, and to declare the truth on the evidence given them in the case. . . . Petty juries, consisting usually of twelve men, attend courts to try matters of fact in civil causes, and to decide both the law and the fact in criminal prosecutions. The decision of a petty jury is called a verdict."

Encourage jurors to write down questions for the judge to pose to each witness during examination and cross-examination.

But in 1895, the Supreme Court held that the failure of the judge to remind the jurors of their powers was not a basis for mistrial or appeal (*Sparf and Hansen* v. *United States*). Although trial by jury is mentioned three times in the Bill of Rights, the definition of trial by jury has changed.

The power of the jury has a long history. William Penn was acquitted by a jury in 1670. His jurors were imprisoned and fined until the highest court of England established that freedom entails a juror's power to vote his conscience. Freedom of the press was established by the Zenger trial in 1735, when a jury acquitted a publisher despite the direction of the judge and the law. Juries refused to enforce the Fugitive Slave Acts in the 1850s. The Fully Informed Jury Association (FIJA) writes that "Recognition of our freedoms of religion, peaceable assembly and speech thus all trace to the exercise of jury power, wielded by juries unintimidated by government judges."[1]

From the Pages of History: Restoring American Justice

Lysander Spooner (1808–87) was a farmer, lawyer, businessman, abolitionist, and civil libertarian.[2] Here is his explanation of the role of juries in a free society, written to encourage jurors to reject the Fugitive Slave Laws of 1850.

For more than six hundred years—that is, since Magna Carta, in 1215—there has been no clearer principle of English or American constitutional law, than that, in criminal cases, it is not only the right and duty of juries to judge what are the facts, what is the law, and what was the moral intent of the accused; but that it is also their right, and their primary and paramount duty, to judge of the justice of the law, and to hold all laws invalid, that are, in their opinion, unjust or oppressive, and all persons guiltless in violating, or resisting the execution of, such laws.

Unless such be the right and duty of jurors, it is plain that, instead of juries being a "palladium of liberty"—a barrier against the tyranny and oppression of the government—they are really mere tools in its hands, for carrying into execution any injustice and oppression it may desire to have executed.

But for their right to judge of the law, and the justice of the law, juries would be no protection to an accused person, even as to matters of fact; for, if the government can dictate to a jury any law whatever, in a criminal case, it

Insist on plain-English instructions to the jury. No legalese.

can certainly dictate to them the laws of evidence. That is, it can dictate what evidence is admissible, and what inadmissible, and also what force or weight is to be given to the evidence admitted. And if the government can thus dictate to a jury the laws of evidence, it can not only make it necessary for them to convict on a partial exhibition of the evidence rightfully pertaining to the case, but it can even require them to convict on any evidence whatever that it pleases to offer them.

"The trial by jury," . . . is a "trial by the country"—that is, by the people—as distinguished from a trial by the government.

The object of this trial "by the country," or by the people, in preference to a trial by the government, is to guard against every species of oppression by the government. In order to effect this end, it is indispensable that the people, or "the country," judge of and determine their own liberties against the government; instead of the government's judging of and determining its own powers over the people. How is it possible that juries can do anything to protect the liberties of the people against the government, if they are not allowed to determine what those liberties are?

Any government, that is its own judge of, and determines authoritatively for the people, what are its own powers over the people, is an absolute government of course. It has all the powers that it chooses to exercise. There is no other—or at least no more accurate—definition of a despotism than this.

On the other hand, any people, that judge of, and determine authoritatively for the government, what are their own liberties against the government, of course retain all the liberties they wish to enjoy. And this is freedom. At least, it is freedom to them; because, although it may be theoretically imperfect, it, nevertheless, corresponds to their highest notions of freedom.

It is supposed that, if twelve men be taken, by lot, from the mass of the people, without the possibility of any previous knowledge, choice, or selection of them, on the part of the government, the jury will be a fair epitome of "the country" at large. . . .

It is fairly presumable that such a tribunal will agree to no conviction except such as substantially the whole country would agree to if they were present, taking part in the trial. A trial by such a tribunal is, therefore, in effect, "a trial by the country." In its results it probably comes as near to a trial by the whole country, as any trial that it is practicable to have, without too great inconvenience and expense. And, if unanimity is required for a conviction, it follows that no one can be convicted, except for the violation of such laws as substantially the whole country wish to have maintained. The government can enforce none of its laws, (by punishing offenders, through the verdicts of juries,) except such as substantially the whole people wish to have enforced. The government, therefore, consistently with the trial by jury, can exercise no powers over the people, (or, what is the same thing, over the accused person, who represents the rights of the people,) except such as substantially the whole people of the country consent that it may exercise. . . .

. . . In short, if the jury have no right to judge of the justice of a law of the government, they plainly can do nothing to protect the people, against the oppressions of the government; for there are no oppressions which the government may not authorize by law.

The jury are also to judge whether the laws are rightly expounded to them by the court. Unless they judge on this point, they do nothing to protect their liberties against the oppressions that are capable of being practiced under cover of a corrupt exposition of the laws. If the judiciary can authoritatively dictate to a jury any exposition of the law, they can dictate to them the law itself, and such laws as they please; because laws are, in practice, one thing or another, according as they are expounded.

The jury must also judge of the laws of evidence. If the government can dictate to a jury the laws of evidence, it can not only shut out any evidence it pleases, tending to vindicate the accused, but it can require that any evidence whatever, that it pleases to offer, be held as conclusive proof of any offense whatever which the government chooses to allege.

The question, then, between trial by jury, as thus described, and trial by the government, is simply a question between liberty and despotism. The authority to judge what are the powers of the government, and what the liberties of the people, must necessarily be vested in one or the other of the parties themselves—the government, or the people; because there is no third party to whom it can be entrusted. If the authority be vested in the government, the government is absolute, and the people have no liberties except such as the government sees fit to indulge them with. If, on the other hand, that authority be vested in the people, then the people have all liberties, (as against the government,) except such as substantially the whole people (through a jury) choose to disclaim; and the government can exercise no power except such as substantially the whole people (through a jury) consent that it may exercise. . . .

The force and justice of the preceding argument cannot be evaded by saying that the government is chosen by the people; that, in theory, it represents the people; that it is designed to do the will of the people; that its members are all sworn to observe the fundamental or constitutional law instituted by the people; that its acts are therefore entitled to be considered the acts of the people; and that to allow a jury, representing the people, to invalidate the acts of the government, would therefore be arraying the people against themselves.

There are two answers to such an argument.

One answer is, that, in a representative government, there is no absurdity or contradiction, nor any arraying of the people against themselves, in requiring that the statutes or enactments of the government shall pass the ordeal of any number of separate tribunals, before it shall be determined that they are to have the force of laws. Our American constitutions have provided five of these separate tribunals, to wit, representatives, senate, executive, jury, and judges; and have made it necessary that each enactment shall pass the ordeal of all these separate tribunals, before its authority can be established by the punishment of those who choose to transgress it. And there is no more absurdity or inconsistency in making a jury one of these several tribunals, than there is in making the representatives, or the senate, or the executive, or the judges, one of them. There is no more absurdity in giving a jury a veto upon the laws, than there is in giving a veto to each of these other tribunals. The people are no more arrayed against themselves, when a jury puts its veto upon a statute, which the other tribunals have sanctioned, than they are when the same veto is exercised by the representatives, the senate, the executive, or the judges.

But another answer to the argument that the people are arrayed against themselves, when a jury holds an enactment of the government invalid, is, that the government, and all the departments of the government, are merely the servants and agents of the people; not invested with arbitrary or absolute authority to bind the people, but required to submit all their enactments to the judgment of a tribunal more fairly representing the whole people, before they carry them into execution by punishing any individual for transgressing them. If the government were not thus required to submit their enactments to the judgment of "the country," before executing them upon individuals—if, in other words, the people had reserved to themselves no veto upon the acts of the government, the government, instead of being a mere servant and agent of the people, would be an absolute despot over the people. It would have all power in its own hands; because the power to punish carries all other powers with it. A power that can, of itself, and by its own authority, punish disobedience, can compel obedience and submission, and is above all responsibility for the character of its laws. In short, it is a despotism. . . .

It is of no avail to say, in answer to this view of the case, that in surrendering their liberties into the hands of the government, the people took an oath from the government, that it would exercise its power within certain constitutional limits; for when did oaths ever restrain a government that was otherwise unrestrained? Or when did a government fail to determine that all its acts were within the constitutional and authorized limits of its power, if it were permitted to determine that question for itself?

Neither is it of any avail to say, that, if the government abuse its power, and enact unjust and oppressive laws, the government may be changed by the influence of discussion, and the exercise of the right of suffrage. Discussion can do nothing to prevent the enactment, or procure the repeal, of unjust laws, unless it be understood that the discussion is to be followed by resistance. Tyrants care nothing for discussions that are to end only in discussion. Discussions, which do not interfere with the enforcement of their laws, are but idle wind to them. Suffrage is equally powerless and unreliable. It can be exercised only periodically; and the tyranny must at least be borne until the time for suffrage comes. Besides, when the suffrage is exercised, it gives no guaranty for the repeal of existing laws that are oppressive, and no security against the enactment of new ones that are equally so. The second body of legislators are liable and likely to be just as tyrannical as the first. If it be said that the second body may be chosen for their integrity, the answer is, that the first were chosen for that very reason, and yet proved tyrants. The second will be exposed to the same temptations as the first, and will be just as likely to prove tyrannical. Who ever heard that succeeding legislatures were, on the whole, more honest than those that preceded them?

When You're Called to Serve . . .

Jury judgment of law can operate only in the direction of mercy. Juries cannot escalate charges or add new charges. That is up to the prosecution and limited by the Constitution. Jurors have the power to reduce charges against the defendant in many cases.

Juries cannot create a law, set precedent, or declare a law to be unconstitutional. These remain the province of the legislature or courts of record. If fully informed juries acquit people accused under a given law, it shows how the country really feels about a law.

As juries become more responsible for conscientiously dispensing justice, prison terms for those convicted of certain crimes will shorten. Typical citizens are concerned about acquitting truly dangerous criminals. They object to crowding prisons with those who are accused of victimless and political crimes.

Most judges will tell you that you may consider "only the facts"—that you are not to let your conscience, your opinion of the law, or the motives of the defendant affect your decision. The judge's task is to referee the trial and provide neutral legal advice to the jury, beginning with a full and truthful explanation of a juror's rights and responsibilities, but judges rarely "fully inform" jurors of their rights. If the judge has qualms about your knowledge of fully informed juries, point out that he assists the prosecution by excusing those jurors who know they have the power to decide if the law itself is just.

Many people don't get fair trials. Too often, jurors apologize to the person they've convicted—or to the community for acquitting when evidence of guilt seems perfectly clear but that evidence has been kept away from the jurors.

Too often, jurors who try to vote their consciences are talked out of it by other jurors who don't know their rights. Some believe they are required to reach a unanimous verdict because "the judge said so."

You cannot be forced to obey a "juror's oath." It is your responsibility to "hang" the jury with your vote if you disagree with the other jurors! Nothing in the U.S. Constitution or in any Supreme Court decision requires jurors to take an oath to follow the laws as the judge explains them. Judges provide their interpretation of the law, but you must think for yourself. Regard all instructions as advice.

If your conscience leads you to hang a jury, you're doing the responsible thing. You cannot be required to reach a verdict. And the jury you hang may be significant as one of a

Fully Informed Jury Association (FIJA)

P.O. Box 59, Helmville, MT 59843; telephone (406) 793-5550.

National Office Hours: 9 A.M.–11 P.M. Mountain Time, most days.

Delivery Address: 1937 Highway 271, Helmville, MT 59843.

Introductory Information toll-free phone line 1-800-TEL-JURY.

- Tell other jurors that they have the power to try the facts and the law without fear of punishment.
- Insist that all participants in the court proceedings must be sworn to tell the truth, especially the lawyers!
- Insist that jurors be selected at random. Only those with a bias should be removed from a jury.
- Ask for jurors to be paid for the value of their time. Involuntary servitude for jurors leads to less qualified panels.
- Court cases are prohibitively expensive. In a civil case, each side's costs ought to be a matter of public record.
- Jurors must be informed of any evidence excluded from trial.

series of hung juries sending messages to the legislature that the law you're working with has problems. It may be time for a change.

More powerful than a voter, more free to speak than a newspaper editor, the American citizen who serves on a jury has the power to veto laws, to solve mysteries, to decide justice. Sadly, this power is almost completely ignored. If you mention this power before you are selected for a jury, you are almost sure to be excluded from the list of potential jurors for a very long time. If you educate your fellow jurors once you are selected, you will do more for liberty than a whole caucus of congressmen.

Juries are primarily an American institution. Experts estimate that 120,000 jury trials are held each year. Ninety percent of these trials are in the United States. The United States is unique because citizens have the right to request a jury trial in most proceedings. Other countries have stopped using the jury system, because it gives power to the people rather than to the authorities.

Yet, even in America, the jury system has been corrupted. Forty-five percent of those summoned to jury service fail to respond. Most law-abiding citizens have thought of excuses to get out of jury service. Judges have kept the power of the jury a secret so long that most people consider jury duty to be nothing short of involuntary servitude.

You are free to obey your conscience as a juror. Some judges may thunder and threaten that fully informed jurors will turn this country from a government of laws into a government of men, but the best judges know that twelve citizens, selected at random, almost always uphold the spirit of the laws. Typical citizens bring a sense of justice to a case that the court insiders can't fathom. No one can punish you for your conduct as a conscientious juror.

What must happen for you to have this power? No new laws are necessary. All you must do is to read —and save—this bagatorial. When you're called for jury duty, be brave and do the decent thing.

If you're an attorney or a judge, check the law on what we've printed. If it's true, start telling the truth to jurors. If this is false or misleading, we challenge you to correct us. And look at the opportunity: jurists who dare to restore the American jury system will win honor and praise.

[1] Fully Informed Jury Association (FIJA) is at P.O. Box 59, Helmville, MT 59843. They would appreciate a donation to cover the cost of mailing; five dollars is probably a fair minimum donation. Much of this information was reprinted from their literature.
[2] Lysander Spooner's collected works are available from Fox & Wilkes, 924 Howard Street, San Francisco, CA 94301.

It's the Devil You Know

Local Government
Is Your Problem

We spend too much money for government. The best estimates say that 47 percent of our National Income goes to government in the form of taxes. Government employees overspend taxes by 5 percent, so the National Debt increases and citizens are poorer. Business is required to spend an additional 10 percent of the National Income to meet government directives.

Most of this money is wasted. Much of it is spent on salaries of people who work to increase their salaries. Many "public servants" work to prevent the rest of us from living happy productive lives. Some are engaged to provide services that ought to be privatized because government is inefficient and unfair. The rest do not care about the common defense, domestic tranquility, or your standard of living. We do what we do despite government.

There is talk about reducing the size and cost of the federal government. It's unlikely to occur, but it's pleasant to contemplate the possibility. Government does not help us to lead happy, healthy lives. Government exists to perpetuate itself.

Unfortunately, even if the federal and state governments were eliminated, we would recover very little freedom. Local governments have grown so big and expensive, with such far-reaching control and power, that local tyrants are shutting down normal economic activity and progress. You do not live in a free country. This causes you to live worse than you should live. And if you're similar to most people, you are oblivious to how you're moving down what Nobel Laureate F.A. Hayek called "The Road to Serfdom."

"Local government is for the locally powerful" stated Arthur Schlesinger in the *Wall Street Journal* in June 1995. Local government has the fewest checks and balances of the three levels of government. Well, it does write a lot of checks, but it is out of control for most people.

Ask yourself:

Q: Who are the locally powerful?

Q: How many people in my community are locally powerful?

Q: Do I know the locally powerful?

Q:Where are the locally powerful?

Q:Am I one of the locally powerful, or am I just one of the rest of the citizens?

Q: Do the locally powerful decide who should lose and who should receive? Who to reward and who to punish?

We operate many stores in many towns, so we have many points of contact with local government. Cities and town can be divided into The Establishment and Everybody Else. The Establishment is usually a very small group of people—less than 1 percent of the population in most cities and counties. Usually less than a dozen people run things, and they run things for their own advantage. The Establishment understands this system. The Establishment plays the system to get what it wants. Different members of The Establishment want different things, so sometimes the locally powerful compete with themselves, but usually they're very close friends.

Politicians want to be somebody. They want power and social recognition. They are more interested in prestige than in money. Money, especially your money, is the means to gratify their egos.

Many are willing to work for years in minor positions as they work their way through the system to a City Council or County Supervisor position. Many of them have always been popular people. In school, they aspired to gain power and prestige. Individually, they are charming, but in groups with other locally powerful folks, they can be dangerous. They will severely damage your well-being in the name of doing good. Most of these people would not do well in a free society, because they can't be satisfied with themselves. If they weren't so invidious, we'd feel sorry for them.

There are usually about a dozen people in elected office in each city. Only three or four have substantial power. Two or three dozen people in each community wait in the wings, trying to act sincere so they can someday "serve the public."

How Local Government Works

We are NOT the People Local Government Employees:

Government employees are in it for the money and the security. They have a good deal. Their organizations grow each year, even though they all complain about "budget cutbacks." They are willing to be subservient to local politicians as long as the politicians reward them with annual increases in pay and benefits. Their egos are rewarded when they interact with private citizens. They play the tyranny of the counter. They know which side they are on, and they see which side you are on.

They show the politicians how to be powerful.

They are rule expanders and rule followers. They are empire builders. They cannot do what makes sense. They cannot use common sense to solve problems. They want to see government expand so their earnings and power will increase. Those at the top play the local game until they run through their bag of tricks. Then they move to a bigger pond and start over. Some of these people might be productive and perform real jobs in a free society. They cost us a lot of money and we are all poorer because of the rules they encourage and enforce. They are practically unaccountable for their actions.

Most of these people mean nothing to The Establishment. Most are foot soldiers. They can say no, but they cannot say yes. They know there are a lot of things they are not going to allow you to do, and they are going to make you wait to do the things you are allowed to do. Only a dozen or so bureaucrats run most organizations. In some places, only one person runs the entire show.

Toadies

These are the most dangerous and destructive people in the political system. Some of them are wannabe politicians, but most of them just want to be part of the process. They want to get invited to parties and functions. They want their friends to know the local politician invited them to serve on an advisory board.

They are eager to be appointed to local commissions and committees. They'll go along with any scheme just to be loved. They ratify. They do not dissent. They rubber-stamp the clever ideas of the staff. They are people with positions that would normally command respect. Politicians use them to fake community support. A few toadies wise up, get disenchanted, and leave the process. The ones that stay destroy civilization. As your freedoms are voted away, meeting by meeting, confiscated, memo by memo, and taxed into oblivion, the toady says "I just wanted to give something back."

There are always enough toadies to meet the need. No meeting is held without at least one toady making a meaningless and inane statement praising the politicians or the process. While pervasive, the number in any community may be limited. Responsible citizens should each make up a toady list for the community. Post it on bulletin boards under the heading "MISSING PRINCIPLES."

Business People

Business people promote their own interests. They are not ideological. They seek advantages. They will generally take short-term benefits at the expense of long-term stability. They'll play the part of the toady if they perceive it to be to their advantage.

They know and respect the power that politicians wield. They calculate the costs politicians can inflict. They pretend to be hurt by the actions of government, and then pass the wasteful cost of bureaucracy on to their customers. They have the facilities necessary to make politicians feel important and powerful. They use these facilities whenever it is to their advantage. They pretend to be capitalists. Capitalism needs to be saved from these business people. They are not defenders or promoters of freedom. Freedom for you is not their objective. Don't rely on business people to save or promote your freedom. As Lenin said, they'll sell you the rope for you to hang them.

Cities and counties have the power and the money to reward business people. They take the money from the non-establishment members of the community. They take the power because no one stands up to the system. Those who play along are well rewarded by the locally powerful. Recalcitrant business people are punished by unequal protection: permits are withheld, fees are levied, and arbitrary regulations are enforced.

We have a corrupt system of local government. There is no difference between paying the right attorney or architect to gain approvals and paying an outright bribe. We operate in a lot of political subdivisions. "Juice" counts if you want to gain local approval and get something done.

Everybody Else

The Establishment represents less than 1 percent of the population. Those are the locally powerful. Either you are part of The Establishment, or you are part of Everybody Else.

The rest of the citizens think someone is handling things. They've either assumed that the system works, or they have become so disenchanted with The Establishment that they've given up. Some of the rest of the citizens just want to run their own lives. They don't have enough points of contact with local government to realize the debilitating effect government has on the community. A few are civically handicapped. They worship through civic religion. They believe that we have the best of all possible systems because that's what they learned in the government school. They don't realize that government steals half of their income, all of their fortunes, and most of their freedom.

The rest of the citizens have everything at stake. The Establishment uses Everybody Else's money and power. Everybody Else needs to realize that voting doesn't work. Voting only gives the sanction of the victim. Government has such great power and funds that it doesn't matter which few people are locally powerful. Only the names of the beneficiaries and the victims change with the names of those in power. Name a time when a change in who held the reins of local power made a difference to Everybody Else.

Everybody Else needs to stop suffering that which is sufferable. They need to take back their money and their power and regain control of their future. Unless this group figures it out and starts saying, "I'm mad as hell and I'm not going to take it anymore," there is no opportunity for freedom.

What You Should Do

1. Take charge of your life and your property. Think of what you can do to make your life better without using force or fraud. Make something. Sell something. Clean something. Fix something. Do it yourself.
2. If you work for the government, quit. You can find a productive job. We realize what you are giving up. We know how hard this will be for you. It's important for you to add to society. To make a contribution, you'll have to work in the private sector.
3. Brighten the corner where you are. Manage yourself. Do something to improve the things you own or manage. Do it today. Worry more about yourself and your own possessions than about other people's possessions and activities. Go the second mile.
4. When you want to help, help someone you know. Help yourself. Help your spouse. Help your children. Help your employees. Help your employer. Help your neighbors. Don't give money to charities. Use that money to help those you know. You can be a powerful force for good, but only for those you know.
5. If you want to give away money or property, make sure it's your own money and your own property you are giving. If we could get The Establishment to live by this one rule, we'd be much better off.
6. Do good voluntarily. Encourage others to do good voluntarily. Don't use the tools of government—force and fraud—to try to do good. If you worry about the means, the ends will take care of themselves.
7. Don't give your sanction to government. Don't honor government or government officials. Try to avoid government-sponsored pageants and spectacles. Participating in the process makes you part of the problem. Resist the temptation to be a knee-jerk statist. You're not so lucky as to live in the best of all possible systems.
8. Never give money to a politician or to a political party. Never help a candidate. Avoid referendums. You are trying to buy something that should not be bought. Money corrupts the political process. It puts a price on freedom. Even if the bad guys spend lots of money, you should keep your wallet closed.
9. Solve your problems yourself. If you need help, persuade those you know to

help you. Try to control your destiny. Don't submit your life for the approval of bureaucrats.

10. Decide what freedom means to you. Decide if you have principles for how you will treat people. The Golden Rule is a great principle: Do Unto Others as You Would Have Them Do Unto You. Stand up for your principles.

11. This is the hardest step of all. Give up something that the government offers to you. Deny yourself some of the promised payoffs of government. Frederic Bastiat wrote that "the State is the great fictitious entity by which everyone expects to live at the expense of everyone else."

12. Resist tyranny. Do everything you can to reduce government and its processes. Develop your own unique methods. Use your personal freedom and responsibility in ways that the government has not imagined. Object to oppression at every opportunity.

13. Shop at Cheaper! We really do sell you more goods for less money. You'll be able to do good for yourself with the money you save.

14. Be happy. Even when you're mad as heck, you still own yourself. Leave it to the locally powerful to be humorless. Live your life so you can declare a victory.

15. Write to us for a list of books about freedom. Our address is "Struggle & Progress," P.O. Box 886, Benicia, CA 94510.

One of the reasons local government costs so much is that local government employees make more money than the rest of the citizens. In addition, they have many more job benefits than most private employees. Typically, they work less, get more time off, take it easy, have greater job security, and get better pensions than nongovernment employees.

A wise man once said, "All expenses come in on two legs." Employee salaries make up two-thirds of the expenditures of most local governments.

Through the Public Access Law, we obtained the W-2 earning of local government employees in four political subdivisions. We then obtained figures from URBAN Decisions on average earning for the same areas.

We estimate that a government pension is worth five times the pension benefits of an average citizen. It's indexed for inflation. Pay is frequently spiked at the end of employment to cause a large pension.

These are not exceptional cases. You will find this true in your local area. Under Public Access Law, cities and counties must give you the W-2 earnings of each employee by name. We suggest you obtain this information for yourself. The code section is Public Records Act (California Government Code 6520 et. seq.). Just mail a letter and ask for the last two years' W-2 earnings broken down by base salary, overtime, deferred compensation, automobile allowance, other pay (which would include situations like acting supervisor pay and vacation buy-back) and the total of all these amounts. Decide for yourself if government employees are overpaid.

Sometimes it is said that a man cannot be trusted with the government of himself. Can he, then, be trusted with the government of others? Or have we found angels in the forms of kings to govern him? Let history answer this question.

A wise and frugal government, which shall restrain men from injuring one another, which shall leave them otherwise free to regulate their own pursuits of industry and improvement, and shall not take from the mouth of labor the bread it has earned; this is the sum of good government.

—*Thomas Jefferson, First Inaugural Address*

Books We Recommend

B*ureaucracy,* by Ludwig von Mises, published by the Center for Futures Education, P.O. Box 489, Cedar Falls, IA 50613 (319) 277-7529.

There is an excess of vanity that is apt to creep upon the people in power in America, who having got out of the crowd, in which they were lost here, upon every little eminency there, think nothing taller than themselves but the trees; and as if there was no after superior judgment to which they should be accountable."

—*William Penn, Letter*

How to Make
Bureaucrats Fear You

Request Public Records and Expose Crimes of Government

Federal and state laws define your right to see and copy government records. Few people realize this right exists. The law states that "access to information . . . is a fundamental and necessary right of every person in this state." Very few realize the effect these laws can have on local government activities.

Local governments in California control over $100 billion in annual spending, according to the Bureau of Census in 1992. They can regulate you out of your home, out of your job, and out of business. They can spend this money and make laws with impunity because there is practically no oversight of local government. Local government is by and for the locally powerful. If you happen to be in the path of the locally powerful, you're out of luck. If you try to hire an attorney, you'll be out of money.

However, you have an interesting alternative. Your right to obtain state and local records is Section 6250 through 6258 of the California Government Code. Your right to obtain federal records is called the Freedom of Information Act. It's Title 5 USCS Section 552. If you want copies of these laws, write to Cheaper! at P.O. Box 886, Benicia, CA 94510, and we'll send them to you.

The California Public Records Act

The Government Code section 6252 defines "public record" as any writing containing information relating to the conduct of the public's business prepared, owned, used, or retained by state or local agencies, regardless of physical form or characteristics. "Writing" includes any means of recording upon any form of communications or representation.

A Public Records Act request is a formal written or spoken request by any person that reasonably describes a record of information. Generally, a city or agency has ten days to determine whether it will comply with a request to produce copies of the record. A government must promptly provide, at no charge, any documents for inspection by the citizen.

A government agency must provide copies of the requested documents. It may charge a fee to cover the cost of duplication. If a government agency denies a request for public records, the notice of denial must state the reason for the denial and the names and titles of each person responsible for the denial. The city or agency is liable for the requestor's court costs and attorney's fees if the court determines that the information should have been disclosed.

The Act applies to all state and local agencies, counties, and cities. Government entities often respond to requests by stating that no specific document responds to the citizen's request. At this point, the citizen should provide a detailed description of the desired information and request the aid of the public records officer in determining which public documents will provide this information.

In addition to the Public Records Act, any individual may request copies of any documents maintained by a California state agency that identifies or describes that individual (Civil Code Sections 1798.1 ti 1798.78).

A Wrench in the Works!

The Freedom of Information Act (FOIA) imposes disclosure obligations on the federal executive branch (other than the Office of the President) and on all independent U.S. agencies. It does not apply to Congress or the U.S. courts. Under the FOIA, any agency must make identifiable nonexempt records promptly available upon request of any person.

FOIA also requires that federal agencies publish in the Federal Register (which is available in the main branch of most city libraries) information describing the agency's control and field organization, its function, procedures, and rules.

Certain government records are exempt from disclosure. However, the exemptions are to be narrowly construed in favor of disclosure. Exemptions include national security or foreign policy matters, documents relating solely to agency internal personnel rules, certain agency memoranda, medical or personal files, law-enforcement investigator files, and trade secrets. All of the exemptions have specific requirements that the government often cannot meet.

The worst feature of the FOIA, distinguishing it from the California Act, is that a federal agency may charge a fee for searching (as well as copying) documents. You know how fast these people work.

In addition to FOIA, the Federal Privacy Act of 1974 allows you access to, and the right to amend inaccurate federal files which concern you (Title 5 USC 7 552A).

Some people worry about world government. Many people worry about the size of the federal government. You can also worry about the state government. The real abuser of power is local government. Confront something you can change.

There are 511,039 elected government office holders. Of these, only 542 are in Washington, D.C.; 18,828 are in the fifty state governments. Of the elected politicians, 491,669 are in 84,955 local governments. This increased by more than 15,000 from the last count, in 1990.

Most contact with the government is local. Most of the frustration we face daily is caused by the intrusive activities of the locally powerful. If we are going to regain personal freedom, we must curtail the nasty tendency to try to run other people's lives. Start by finding the new restrictions politicians and bureaucrats are putting into law. Use the Public Records act!

The city or state agency may try to deny you the information. It may postpone producing the information. It may ignore you. It may try to bully you.

Some government officials will try to thwart you in your attempt to get information about their activities. They will try to browbeat you into dropping your request. We are often stonewalled in our legitimate requests for information.

It goes something like this:

1. We send a letter requesting specific information or documents.
2. The official to whom the letter is sent ignores the request.
3. We remind the official that the code requires the information be submitted within a ten-day period.
4. The official states the matter is complex. "It will take extra time," he says.
5. Sometimes they state they aren't required to supply the information. Sometimes they deny the law exists. Sometimes they misquote the law. So we threaten to file an action to force them to fulfill our request.
6. At this point, we consult an attorney. Government attorneys aren't very well versed on these code sections. They don't realize they must supply the information no matter how much they detest doing so.

Do You Want to Know . . .

1. What were the actual W-2 (gross wages) earnings for every employee in the city? What were they actually paid last year? How much did they earn in overtime?
2. What is the contract for your school superintendent or your city manager? What about the football coach at the University of California? The professor who hardly ever shows up at your local community college? What are the goodies, the spiffs, and the secret deals?

3. Did you want to see your permanent record? Copies of all your school records, including comments from your teachers, your grades, and your aptitude test scores are public records.
4. Who has sued a government agency? What was it about, and how much was the settlement? What did the city attorney tell the city council about the lawsuit during the closed council meetings?
5. What is the pension plan for local employees? How much more can they take out of your pocket?
6. What contracts has the city made with companies? What's in the franchise agreement between the city and the trash company? What deal has the city made with the publc utility?
7. How many trips has the city council taken? How much did they spend on travel? How much were they reimbursed for entertainment and business expenses? What does each council member own?
8. How much was contributed to each candidate? What does each politician own? Who gives out the money? How is the money laundered?
9. How much money was spent on each school?
10. What records does the government keep on you? What did the council member write in her taxpayer-purchased diary about you?
11. Who are the tax delinquents? What does the detailed budget say? What really happened at that meeting you missed?
12. How much compensatory time has each and every government employee accumulated? What will that accumulation eventually cost the government agency?
13. Who has the city discharged in the last five years? Who has retired? Who retired after service and who retired because of a disability? Which employees used the tax exemption for disability to increase their pension?
14. What work do city employees actually do? When do they work? Why do they say, "We are understaffed!"?
15. What gratuities were received by employees during 1992, 1993, and 1994?
16. How much do toll takers earn? How many tolls are lost to theft by toll takers?

We successfully obtained the W-2 salary figures for each member of the Sacramento Police Department. We wrote the city for the information citing the Public Records Act. City attorneys stated that they did not have to supply the information.

We filed suit in superior court and the judge ruled in our favor. The Sacramento Police Officers Association filed an appeal in appellate court. The appeal was denied. The city supplied the wage information and the judge awarded The Customer Company $8,000 for legal fees.

Public salaries are the public's business. Salaries are more than half of local government expenditures. Government employee salaries and benefits are out of control. Politicians have lost control of these salaries. If we are to rein in the cost of government, we must lower government salary costs to the levels earned by private citizens. To control salaries we must first know the details.

If once the people become inattentive to public affairs, you and I and Congress and Assemblies, Judges and Governors, shall all become wolves. It seems to be the law of our general nature, in spite of individual exceptions.

Certain forms of government are better calculated than others to protect individuals in the free exercise of their natural rights, and are at the same time themselves better guarded against degeneracy, yet experience has shown that even under the best forms, those entrusted with power have in time, and by slow operations, perverted into tyranny.

—*Thomas Jefferson*

Publicity is justly commended as a remedy for social and industrial diseases. Sunlight is said to be the best of disinfectants; electric light the most efficient policeman.

—*Louis Brandeis, "Other People's Money"*

February 14, 1995

Dr. Annette O'Conner, Superintendent
Benicia Unified School District
350 East K
Benicia, California 94510

Dear Superintendent O'Conner:

We would like to know the following information about your School District:
    For all employees, by name, we request documents describing their 1993 and 1994 actual earnings broken down by base salary, overtime, deferred compensation, automobile allowance, other pay (which would include situations like acting supervisor pay, vacation buy back), and the total of all these amounts.
    In addition, we are requesting documents that provide, by name, the following information:

1. Length of employment for each employee.
2. Position held.

3. Grade/level now held in the position (if applicable) by employee.
4. A listing of grades by position in your district, including the range of base salary for each grade level in each position.
5. Requirements to move from one grade/level to the next.

I am also requesting documents providing the following information on your school district's retirement plan:

1. What percentage of pay does each employee contribute?
2. What percentage does the school district contribute for all employees?
3. Please prepare for all employees.
4. Please prepare a copy of your retirement plan.

I am also requesting documents describing benefits on the following programs in your school district:

1. Vacation
2. List of days considered holidays
3. Sick leave
4. Compensatory time
5. Any other approved time off

I would like to know this information for all times of employment service.

Each of the above requests is a separate request for records under the Public Records Act, Cal. Gov't. Code 6250, et. seq. Please let me know when the material is available. I will pick it up and pay any copying charges.

Very truly yours,

Jay Chapman

December 15, 1994

Los Angeles City Board of Education
Region A
1208 Magnolia Avenue
Gardena, California 90247

Gentlemen:

I attended public school in Gardena. I attended Purche Elementary School in Gardena from September, 1959 through June, 1986. I attended Henry Clay Junior High School from September, 1966 to June, 1969. I attended Gardena High School from September, 1969 to June, 1972.

My address during that entire time was 2916 West 136th Street, Gardena, California 90249. My parents are Ina and Yale Chapman.

I would like to receive a copy of all my school records from all three schools. This would include all files, records, permanent files, and permanent records you have for me.

This is a request for records under the Public Records Act Ca. Gov't. Code 6250, et. seq. I am enclosing a check for $10.00 to cover copying and mailing costs. Please send the information to 4457 Park Road, Benicia, California 94510.

Very truly yours,

Jay Chapman

Decriminalize Drugs!

A dime spent on drug enforcement is a dime wasted.
Think of the billions spent on the "War on Drugs" as a subsidy to crime.

Why? The war on drugs is already lost. "Let's call off the war and make the best of the peace. . . . It's a lot easier to sweep up gutters than to fight a hopeless war," writes Mike Royko, Pulitzer Prize–winning columnist with the *Chicago Tribune*. Royko points out that there aren't enough prisons to hold all the users and dealers. There could never be enough prisons.

"What would make still more sense would be to admit that we are not God, that we cannot live other people's lives or save people who don't want to be saved, and to take the profits out of drugs by decriminalizing them. That is what destroyed the bootlegger gangs after Prohibition was repealed," writes Thomas Sowell, noted economist and senior fellow with the Hoover Institution at Stanford.

Current policy is a failure. "Cocaine users have created the largest, most vicious criminal enterprise the world has ever known," says Colombian President Virgilio Barco. Drug money corrupts law enforcement. Thanks to the Drug Prohibition, Colombian drug dealers are the richest men in the world. They can pay off enough law enforcement to get their product distributed, no matter how intense the "War on Drugs."

Experts estimate that 60 percent of crime is drug-related. Building a criminal-justice system strong enough to hold back drugs is impossible. Even prisoners in federal penitentiaries deal drugs!

Drug use is, like it or not, legal or not, an individual choice. Each of us decides for himself. Where did this "War on Drugs" come from? Puritans, Prohibitionists, and oligarchs masquerading as concerned public servants. How many billion dollars do they want to spend? What a waste! Drugs are bad—no question about that. Why, Prohibition makes them worse!

Users must realize that actions have consequences. Putting users in jail isn't working, won't work, can't work. Instead, stop treating users as victims. Stop paying for drug-rehabilitation programs. The drug user is no victim. The drug user must be responsible for his own treatment! Good citizens who don't use drugs are the casualties of the "War on Drugs." Decriminalization means the start of liberation for drug-free citizens.

Well, what do you think? Mail your comments to: Cheaper!, P.O. Box 886, Benicia, CA 94510.

Our trouble in drugs comes from prohibiting drugs, just as our trouble in alcohol in the 1920s was from the Prohibition of alcohol. We finally had the sense to repeal Prohibition in 1934. We won't get a handle on the drug problem until we repeal prohibition of drugs. Don't misunderstand me, drugs are terrible. It is a shame and a disgrace that so many of our young people use drugs. But the way we are going about it is wrong; we are not stopping the influence of drugs but only making them expensive. We are producing widespread violence, crime, and corruption of our legal enforcement machinery. We are interfering with our relations with foreign countries and our foreign policy without doing anything. There are two classes of victims of drugs—those who take drugs and those who do not. If drugs had been legalized 15 or 20 years ago, crack would never have existed. Crack was invented because prohibition makes the usual and less harmful kind of drugs so expensive. You would not have these gang wars among youths in Los Angeles or elsewhere, where people have been killed. If drugs were legalized, initially more people would use them. But they would be harming themselves. What are our law enforcement officers doing? Estimates are that 60 percent of violent crimes are related to drugs.

What is the correct posture for the U.S. Government to insure that current economic changes in communist countries keep moving forward? Set them a good example by doing what we profess to believe in. We profess to believe in human freedom, and what we do every day is to restrict human freedom in one way or another. This is still one of the freest countries in the world. We are very fortunate. Can we keep it that way? Not unless we change our policy.

Excerpted from Nobel Prize–winning economist Milton Friedman's remarks made to The Commonwealth Club of California, on July 21, 1989. Remarks used with permission of The Commonwealth Club.

BAGATORIALS

ABOUT THE EMPEROR'S NEW CLOTHES

America's Medical System Is Changing ... from Bad to Worse

First, confuse the Vocabulary.

Disease threatens medicine in America. Worse than cancer, worse than heart disease, worse than a horrible, crippling accident, the political plans of powerful government officials threaten the health of America. During the past year, the Clintons have captured the debate over America's medical care. They plan to socialize the medical system of the United States. They have advanced ideas, pulled them back, organized task forces, held massive "secret" meetings, and fueled speculation. Over and over, the Clintons have promised plans and then postponed announcements. To some, they seem inept. In truth, the Clintons have captivated the media. The Clintons control the debate on how you can be cured.

Look at the language. Americans now believe there is a "health-care crisis." The Clintons' prescriptions are described with a vocabulary few understand. Reports of the plan have been illustrated with stories calculated to induce nationwide hypochondria. This masterful propaganda campaign has enough people fooled enough of the time for the Clintons to have a free hand in restructuring this trillion-dollar activity. Their choice is socialism.

Lenin's instruction was "First, confuse the vocabulary." The Clintons have done that. As Rose Wilder Lane wrote,

> Thinking can be done only in words. Accurate thinking requires words of precise meaning. Communication between human beings is impossible without words whose precise meaning is generally understood. Confuse the vocabulary, and millions are helpless against a small, disciplined number who know what they mean when they speak.

Here are some of the terms used in the medical care debate: managed care, managed competition, provider networks, health-insurance purchasing corporations, play or pay, health alliances, health care, single-payer system, individual mandate. Acronyms include

CLIA, RBRVS, OSHA, PPS, DRGS, PROS, PPRC, and MVPS. Only the insiders know what they think they're talking about. Since they control the terms, they control the debate. The medical community and the public have been excluded from the debate. What they're debating is your freedom.

Is the Medical System Broken?

Eighty-one percent of Americans are "satisfied with the quality of health care for themselves and their families," said a Gallup poll in mid-May.[1]

Compare that with American's satisfaction with any government-run system or service. Who helps you more—your doctor or the typical public-school teacher? Which encourages better behavior—your doctor or the welfare system? Where do you get help faster—at your doctor's or at the post office? Who works harder—your doctor or any city employee? Which is more effective—America's medical system or America's criminal-justice system?

The Clintons talk about waste in medicine. They talk about saving a lot of money by cutting out inefficiency. Bureaucratic medicine, especially government-administered bureaucracy, is inherently inefficient and expensive, yet the Clintons aim to solve the problem by putting the rest of medicine under government control. Let the Clintons first show us some results in the activities government now controls and mismanages. The campaign to "reinvent government" is the tenth presidential campaign this century to fix the problems of bureaucracy. It's a sham.

Why Socialize Medicine?

The Clintons are Fabian[2] socialists. They believe the government can run people's lives better than people can run their own lives. Forty-five percent of the U.S. Gross National Product, the total of all goods and services produced in the country, is socialized. Forty-five percent of what we produce is spent according to the dictates of politicians and bureaucrats. A good share of these resources are frittered away. The personal initiative of many Americans has been stifled. We are all poorer for it.

The government estimates that the U.S. medical system is 14 percent of the Gross National Product. Socializing medicine is the biggest bite the Clintons can take to

> Socialism: 1 : any of various economic and political theories advocating collective or governmental ownership and administration of the means of production and distribution of goods 2 a : a system of society or group living in which there is no private property b : a system or condition of society in which the means of production are owned and controlled by the state.[3]

increase the size of government. Their plan is a takeover of the entire sector— many are convinced there is no other choice. Danger! Socialized medicine will mean you receive a lower quality of medical care. You'll give up more of your income and more of your property. You'll also give up some personal freedom.

Will Medicine Be Free?

Of course not. Some people think government-mandated medical care will be free to them. They know the government doesn't do anything well, but this plan seems to give them something for nothing. Politicians use greed to sell socialism. They know most of you won't pay attention to the cost.

Medical care will actually become more expensive. The government has no money of its own. The government spends what it takes from you and me. You'll pay in higher taxes. You'll pay in lower wages. You'll pay in time spent waiting for treatment. You'll pay in time spent waiting for bureaucracy to function. You'll pay for government waste. You'll pay to go outside the country for the treatment you need.

Medical care is now paid for as part of people's wages. Dr. Milton Friedman relates the history of how the government limited wage increases during the 1940s. Since employers couldn't raise wages to attract employees, business started to pay for medical care. The IRS moved to tax medical benefits, but was rebuffed. Companies buy medical care in bulk with pretax dollars.

The Clintons want to end this system. They want to tax the cost of medical benefits. Roughly 7 percent will be added to your payroll taxes to pay the medical costs of those who do not have medical insurance. You will pay your own costs, plus the costs of those who do not have insurance (either because they do not work or because they do not pay their own costs). If you work for a living, your personal cost for medical care will increase.

"This is going to require a degree of discipline that people aren't used to," says Michael Dukakis, the former governor of Massachusetts. "Millions of Americans make their own diagnoses and then go from doctor to doctor. They're spoiled."[4]

Welcome to socialized medicine! Would you like some postage stamps with that cough medicine?

Who Can't Get Medical Care Today?

No one. Although no one's medical care is as good as it could be (except President Clinton's), everyone receives treatment today. Our system provides care and passes on the cost to those who pay for medical care. Doctors, nurses, and medical suppliers provide a great deal of free care and volunteer care. Hospitals are required to provide treatment. It is a newsworthy scandal when a patient is refused.

Socialists argue that 14 percent of the population is uninsured, so 14 percent lack medical care. So who are the thirty-seven million uninsured Americans?[5] Since the poor are covered by Medicaid, and the old are covered by Medicare, they are neither the old nor the poor. A Congressional Budget Office survey found that 51 percent of the uninsured are uninsured for four months or less; 72 percent of the uninsured find insurance within a year.

Expect quality of care to suffer

Twenty-seven percent of the uninsured (about ten million people) have family incomes over $30,000 per year. Many are young and well-educated people who choose not to have medical insurance. Instead, they pay for medical bills as the charges are incurred. Many of the uninsured do what we all do in a free-market economy. They look at the alternatives and decide to spend their money as they see fit. They may choose something besides medical insurance. Some of the uninsured plan to receive treatment at free clinics.[6]

California has mandatory automobile financial-responsibility requirements. The Department of Motor Vehicles reports that 20 percent of the state's drivers do not have automobile insurance. Compare this with the 14 percent who lack medical insurance.

Skeptical? Check the Congressional Budget Office report. You'll see we don't have a medical-care crisis. What we have is an opportunity for socialists to sweep an additional 14 percent of the economy into the hands of the politically powerful.

What Does the Government Run Well?

Why does anyone think the government will run the medical system better than people run it for themselves? Medical practitioners say most of what ails the system is the result of government rules and regulations. The big-jackpot court system adds to those costs. Worst of all, no one can point out something the government runs well now.

Consider Three Large Government Programs

Public safety: The police, the courts, and the prisons are run by the government. Are you safe? Are you protected from theft, violence, and fraud? Government spends more and more on police, on prisons, and on the courts every year, yet our lives become more and more dangerous.

Poverty: The government has spent billions to reduce poverty. Has the government taken poverty out of the people? The welfare system is corrupt. It spends more on administration than on assistance to the needy. It encourages deceit and sloth.

Public education: Education has been compulsory since 1900. Bureaucrats squander vast sums on public schools, yet schoolchildren know less than their counterparts from fifty years ago. Quality of education is inverse to the government involvement and spending.

To expect socialized medicine to improve the quality of medical care is illogical. To hope for government intervention to help cure individuals is irrational. To think the Clintons' plans will be beneficial is insane.

How Much Is Too Much Medical Care?

Government statistics say Americans spend 14 percent of the GNP on medical care. Is that too much? Most of the industrialized world spends 9 percent. The Clintons argue that the additional 5 percent spent by Americans makes us "uncompetitive." They want to capture the 5 percent and spend it on their social programs.

If you're sick, you couldn't care less what percent of the GNP it will cost to cure you. It's up to you to decide how much to spend to get the best medical care. Do you want a bureaucrat making the decision for you?

Most of us should spend more time and money making ourselves healthier. Our bodies are our basic property rights. We own ourselves. We're never broke as long as we stay alive. Healthy people manage their own health and fitness. Sick people recover when they find the cure that works for them. Should bureaucrats decide how many times you can see a doctor? Should government standards dictate the treatment? Even with socialized medicine, if you want to be well, you'll have to write your own prescription for health. If the government obstructs your choice, you'll be sicker.

If Americans freely decide to spend 20 percent of the GNP on their health, should officials be allowed to prohibit the expenditure?

What Government Medicine Will Mean

- More bureaucracy. Our present system is hindered by government rules and interference. Any new system will be a nightmare of mandates, rules, and regulations. Individuals ought to be more involved and more responsible for their own medical care—government medicine will restrict an individual's choices.
- More cost. Government medicine will cost society more rather than less. Government medicine will require more administration. More regulation. More paperwork.
- Less service. Russell Means, the Indian leader, says, "You want a national health care system? Come on down to the reservation and I'll show you what that's like. . . . Wake up America or you'll become part of the reservation."[7]
- Slower progress. Bureaucracies do not foster medical breakthroughs. Discoveries come from free men acting in unconventional ways to solve a mystery. Bureaucracy stifles innovation.
- Fewer choices. Many illnesses are cured when patients take their problems into their own hands. Many people search out the most plausible diagnosis by reading and challenging several doctors. They search out treatment. Choice of doctors and treatment cannot be delegated away. You care more about your health than anyone else. You could quite easily become a victim of systemization.

You may not be able to choose your own doctor.

What's Good Medicine?

You must be able to choose your own doctor. You must be able to investigate and approve the selection of treatment. You must be able to decide how much medical care you need and how much you can afford. You must be able to change doctors and medical-care facilities.

You ought to be treated like a customer. Medicine must not be managed like the post office. You ought to be able to find a doctor who cares how you feel. Doctors must treat patients with respect. There ought to be enough competition for doctors to choose to be punctual, informed, courteous, and concerned.

Doctors ought to be able to design their practices themselves, without regulations and expensive dispute-settlement systems. Doctors ought to be able to drive their costs low enough so doctors can afford to make house calls again.

If you want to buy the best possible care, you ought to be able to buy the best possible care—if you can pay for it. "Really good care" is within reach of ordinary people in a market system. Charity, not socialism, must and will provide for those who cannot afford their own care. In fact, charity will provide better care than socialism. This charity happens even now.

What's Bad Medicine?

Controls on medical or drug costs are bad for your health. Price controls lead to shortages and rationing. Price controls restrict services and stop innovation.

A "national ceiling" on medical expenditures is bad for your health. People must ration their own medical expenditures.

More taxes are bad for your health. What you spend yourself is spent wisely; what you give to the government to spend is wasted. Everyone already receives treatment now. Additional taxes will restrict your choices.

Socialism is bad for your health. People in free countries are healthier than people in socialist or fascist countries. Socialism is good for the powerful, and bad for everyone else.

Our Prescription

Medical insurance ought to be bought like other types of insurance. Use medical insurance for catastrophic expenditures. Turning every expense in to an insurance company is inefficient and costly. We pay in this bureaucratic fashion so that our medical expenses are paid with pretax dollars. Bureaucracy, both public and private, would be cut if all medical expenses were tax-deductible, even if no insurance company was involved. If tax revenues went down and government spending was restricted, you would be richer.

There ought to be a charge for every medical procedure. The world's rule is "If it's free, take it." At zero cost, demand is infinite. The keys to containing medical costs are prudent living, individual responsibility, the support from families, and a recognition that life is terminal. People make these decisions well now; their ability to decide should be respected. Bills ought to be simple to read. The doctor ought to take the time to explain the charges.

Medicine should be deregulated. People are protected from quacks and miracle cures by good sense. Government approval gives people a false sense of security. A physician's concern for his or her good reputation is what really protects you from phony cures. A market system demands and rewards the good faith, goodwill, good ethics, and good intentions of medical practitioners. Good behavior cannot be regulated. If the government could dictate good behavior, federal penitentiaries would be pleasant places.

Recognize risk. Doctors must be free to practice medicine as best they can. Prior to treatment, patient and physician should agree to binding arbitration to solve any disputes that may arise. The doctor's primary concern must be to maintain or restore the health of the patient. It's difficult to concentrate when one's attention is devoted to limiting one's liability.

Details of Clinton's health plan will change between the time we wrote this bag and the time you read it. In fact, changes will occur as the plan is presented to the Congress, during the hearings, during the House-Senate conference, and as the regulations are written after the signing. The debate will become so complicated that none can follow it. Actually, even if you could follow it, there's nothing you could do to stop this socialist juggernaut. What you'll have to do is figure out a way to get medical coverage despite the inefficiencies of socialized medicine. Good luck.

[1]Martin Anderson, *Plain Dealer,* May 26, 1993.
[2]*The National Encyclopedia,* 1932, vol. 4, p. 237: "an important Socialist organization in England, founded in 1883 ... The Fabians believed that Socialism could in large measure be adopted and evolved, through the agency of existing parties. They urged the nationalization of land and such industries as could be conveniently managed socially, and they worked also for the amelioration of social conditions. They took their name from the Roman Fabius, with his policy of victory by delay."
[3] *Webster's New Collegiate Dictionary,* 1977, p. 1102.
[4]Reported by George Anders in "Visits to Doctor's Office Will Be Different," *Wall Street Journal,* September 13, 1993.
[5]Congressional Budget Office and Employee Benefit Research Institute study of census data, as reported by Martin Anderson, *Plain Dealer,* May 26, 1993. Beware of any number you don't make up yourself.
[6]James P. Weaver, "The Best Care Other People's Money Can Buy," *Wall Street Journal,* November 19, 1992. A physician relates the story of a patient who receives $275,000 in care but balks at a $75 charge for dentures because the patient must pay the $75 himself.
[7]Reported by Matt Peiken, *Fairfield Daily Republic,* April 9, 1993.

Will You Own Yourself?

by Wendy McElroy

Although I am Canadian, I've been treated by doctors in the United States and at home. I am astounded that Americans look north for a model to imitate. The expense alone should make Americans tremble: despite its comparatively minuscule defense spending and high taxes, Canada has a higher per-capita deficit than the States. Single-payer health care is expensive.

Meanwhile, Canadians queue up for lifesaving operations. If they are rich and prominent, they seek treatment in America. Sometimes patients are routed southward simply because state-of-the-art medical care is scarce in Canada. Rationing affects more than life-saving operations or extraordinary measures. My doctor recently refused to rerun an inexpensive blood test.

Clinton's health plan contains most of the flaws of the Canadian system. It replaces the wisdom of the marketplace with the edicts of bureaucrats. The plan will pass in some form, because Clinton has shrewdly bribed many of the powerful who might have opposed him. Big businesses (such as auto manufacturers) may be promised lower costs for the health care of retired employees. Labor may be promised generous health-insurance subsidies to cover early retirement. Veterans may be assured that a renovated health system will serve them better. Seniors may hear about new Medicare benefits. The truth is, you will pay much, much more. We all can't get something for nothing.

It's a long way to Acapulco.

What Is the Clinton Plan?

Five hundred health-care experts schemed behind closed doors for four months in order to draft the 1,342-page proposed health plan. Few people know what's going on. The basics of the plan are:

- A standard health-care package available to every American, at least in theory. Employees and individuals won't select the coverage they prefer. They must accept what the government offers.
- A National Health Board to design the package. This will be a political body, subject to political pressure. Power will be transferred from individuals to the government. For example, people will be assigned to doctors. You won't be able to keep searching for the diagnosis and cure that work for you.
- New institutions, known as health alliances, will provide health care to regions of the country. These semigovernment agencies will join health care providers into one gigantic bureaucracy.
- A firm ceiling on health-care spending: $1,800 per individual and $4,200 per family. Business will pick up 80 percent of this cost, government 20 percent.
- A pledge that no new taxes will be necessary to pay for the health plan—beyond a tobacco tax, of course.

Clinton wants to restructure an industry that constitutes 14 percent of the U.S. economy and which touches every American. He wishes to place everyone's health under government control. Doctors who refuse to join a government-managed health unit will be strictly regulated. And for those who wish to escape being socialized, a ceiling will be set on private as well as public health-care spending.

The Clinton plan is the most expansive domestic policy since Franklin Roosevelt pushed through the New Deal. And it is a fraud.

There Is No Health Crisis

The current system is already required to provide everyone with medical care. Hospitals must, by law, treat people regardless of their ability to pay. What Clinton conceals is that many uninsured are simply young and healthy people who prefer to pay medical expenses as incurred. Or they use alternative medicine. Or free clinics.

The fact is—despite AIDS and runaway crime—Americans are healthier than ever. Life expectancy has increased from sixty-eight years in 1950 to seventy-six years in 1992. Polls show Americans are content with their medical care. According to a recent Time/CNN poll, 78 percent are satisfied. A *Wall Street Journal* poll found that 73 percent have no major complaint. A Mellman & Lazarus poll reported that 61 percent think the system meets their needs. In a Time/CNN national poll conducted immediately after Clinton's 1993 State of the Union message, less than 1 percent of Americans picked health care as the main problem facing the country today.

Fill out these forms and call us in the morning.

Where is the crisis in health care? Especially when compared with the crisis in the economy? The panic revolves around the roughly thirty-seven million who lack health insurance. In fact, only about 5.5 million Americans lack coverage for two years or more, because they don't get jobs with health benefits and they don't qualify for Medicaid. These are the same people most likely to fall through the cracks of Clinton's job-based plan. They are unlikely to gain more access to sophisticated health care than they have now. Middle-class Americans fear losing their health insurance. They fear disastrous medical bills. Americans like medical care, but they want it to be more affordable.

Ironically, one of the reasons medical care is so expensive is that it keeps people alive. "Halfway technologies"—like kidney dialysis—allow people who would have died to function, but offer no cure. This increases the number of elderly and infirm people, who require intensive care. Rationing might mean death to these expensive patients.

Americans classify more and more services under the heading of health care. Only a few decades ago, mental health was narrowly defined to include people who could not function in society. Today, most people with a mental illness suffer from "character disorders." They function well despite phobias, compulsions, eating disorders, and the like. A lot of surgery is not aimed at curing a disease. Many knee operations are performed to keep the patient on the golf course or ski slopes. When you keep expanding the definition of health, you expand the costs as well.

Nevertheless, these factors don't explain why health care has risen at three to four times the rate of inflation.

The Real Reason for the High Cost of Health Care

Any cure begins with an accurate diagnosis.

For more than twenty-five years, patients have been shielded from the true cost of health care because it appeared that someone else paid the bills. The tax code masks the "real" cost of health care, because employers deduct their health-insurance plans and employees do not see the bills. (Individuals receive no tax break on any insurance they buy.) The proposed health system is a government attempt to avoid the most basic of economic laws:

Prices rise when demand increases. Demand increases when prices fall.

Government has failed miserably. Yet people look to government for solutions. Clinton tells people what they want to hear: "You can have the best medical care in the world at no cost." Behind the pleasant rhetoric lies an ugly truth. Every American will be required to use a standard insurance package that includes services most of them will never use and would never buy for themselves.

What Benefits Does the Clinton Plan Claim to Offer?

Claim #1: Medical care will be cheaper.

Clinton says he can pay the $441-billion tab for his health-care plan through cost-cutting and marginal tax increases, including a 1-percent tax on corporations that opt for their own health plan. But two-thirds of the estimated savings come from unspecified "systems" savings. All estimates are based on keeping medical costs under control.

On what does he base this? Medicare and Medicaid have both grown at three or four times the rate of inflation. The nation's health budget has soared from 5.9 percent of GDP in 1965 to 14 percent in 1992. And as the baby-boomers age, medical care will become more expensive.

A few businesses like the Clinton plan, because the government claims the plan will assume most of the costs for aging employees. The real burden will shift to taxpayers. Small businesses may also cut jobs to pay higher insurance premiums. The National Federation of Independent Businesses estimates that smaller businesses will have to cut between 400,000 and 1.5 million jobs in the first year.

Clinton claims expenses will be held down by cutting back on paperwork. When my husband and I moved to Canada, we opted to pay a $59-a-month fee for health insurance that covered both of us. (Since Ontario prohibits private practice, it is difficult to pay bills as they arise.) A few years ago, the government refused to take our money. The reason? It costs them more to process the few hundred thousand checks they received each month than to extend free coverage to everyone. It is difficult to imagine a business losing money by getting too many checks, but somehow government managed it. This is the bureaucracy Clinton uses as an example of an efficient single provider of health care. It's ludicrous.

In the end, the only way the government can hold down health costs is to deny treatment to some people by rationing.

Claim #2: There will be greater access to health care.

At zero cost, demand for any product or service is unlimited. Imagine that health care is an "all-you-can-eat" buffet with no admission price. It is bound to be overused.

Currently, the healthiest 50 percent of Americans account for about 3 percent of health-care spending each year. The sickest 1 percent account for about 30 pecent. As more and more healthy people demand the totally free services to which they are "entitled," services will be restricted by rationing. Or by providing worse service. Or by both. The people who suffer will be the very ill who require the most expensive care. Government committees will weigh the cost of a lifesaving operation against the cost to immunize children against the flu. As price controls cause shortages, rationing will become more severe.

Claim #3: Health care will be fair.

Clinton's health plan is supposed to protect the poor. Actually, the wait for health care will become longer. A few people may escape to foreign countries for special care, if they can afford it. Those who must stay in the U.S. will receive worse care and less care.

The real transfer of wealth is from those who are healthy to those who are not. It is a transfer that ignores the income of both parties, as well as the reason for illness (such as willful drug abuse). The poor may seem to win under this plan but, like the elderly, they would initially remain covered by Medicaid and Medicare—both of which have been targeted for strenuous cost-cutting.

The bottom line is that upcoming generations—your children and grandchildren—will be shackled with the cost of providing health care for aging baby-boomers, many of whom will be affluent. Does this sound fair?

Then What Is the Solution?

The real alternative is the free market, in which individuals choose for themselves. In the free market, the price of medical care would fall to the price people are willing to pay for it. Health-care providers would compete to provide better, cheaper care, just as we compete to provide better, cheaper food. The cost of medical care limits how much people use. It is an incentive to stay healthy.

Medical insurance, like car or house insurance, should be bought to cover only catastrophic expenses. Just as auto insurance does not pay for oil checks, neither should medical insurance pay for routine services, such as annual physicals. Ninety percent of health care is directed at noncrisis situations, in which patients can shop for the best deal. Competition keeps costs down. Malpractice insurance, which raises the cost of health care for everyone, should be replaced by binding arbitration.

When you walk into a doctor's office, you should agree with the doctor to go to arbitration in case of a dispute. Both of you will save time, money, and aggravation, especially if awards are limited to predetermined and mutually agreeable limits.

Medical Saving Accounts, which allow people to self-insure against noncatastrophic expenses, should become as common as IRAs. If the money set aside is not taxable, accumulate it in an interest-bearing account until needed. All medical insurance must be tax-deductible.

Individuals ought to care for family members in their own homes, rather than making society (other individuals) assume the burden. Discarding elderly or infirm relatives into state homes is a recent, disturbing trend.

Doctors and hospitals must advertise and compete with each other to provide the widest range of services at the lowest price. Competition encourages such niceties as simple, readable bills and courteous service.

Alternative medicine ought to compete in the marketplace on the same level as the AMA orthodoxy. Doctors and hospitals should not have the advantages of subsidized medicine or licenses that restrict others. The best protections anyone can have against quacks and miracle cures are common sense, personal recommendations, and the reputation of the health-care provider.

New technologies should be publicized and sought out for use. These breakthroughs can revolutionize the cost and quality of medical care. For example, telemedicine now allows specialists a continent away to examine patients in a small rural clinic. This is the marketplace moving with an antibureaucratic speed and precision.

You'll have lots of time to dream.

In a free market, good health care is within the reach of most people. Good medicine requires freedom of choice, including the freedom to choose your own doctor and to demand second and third opinions. Good medicine must include new treatments and techniques. By contrast, the Clinton plan subjects all medical progress to bureaucratic and political approval. If it passes, you will have to work much harder to be healthy.

Your body is who you are. The care of your body must be under your control. You alone know the sort of health care which can help you live as you desire.

Telling you how much to spend on health care is like telling you how to educate your children. Only you can decide. Anyone who tries to decide for you is trying to control you. That's bad for you.

You should start to think about how you will maintain good health if America's quality of care deteriorates. Start off with the basics: Do what makes sense with your diet. Exercise, to build both strength and endurance. Sleep well every night. Try to get along with the people you deal with. When you are sick or injured, get treatment quickly. Don't trust your doctor. Caveat patient.

You may lose your ability to shop around for the best care, so you may want to learn to speak Spanish. The best doctors in North America may be in Mexico, because the last free market in medicine may be in Acapulco or Mexico City.

How CHP Officers Bilk Us

O ne day, he's racing down the freeway on his Harley, a vigorous California Highway Patrol officer in hot pursuit of a speeder. The next day, he's "disabled," sitting in the sun and collecting a fat, tax-free pension check.

"Oh my," you say, "that officer must have been run over by a drunk driver or maybe even shot by a drug-crazed thug. He's another victim of our violent society."

Sorry, you've got it backward. This highway patrolman is a winner, not a loser. The real victim in this story is you . . . and all the other people who pay taxes to the state of California. You're financing a fraud-infested pension system that pays off for everyone from humble motorcycle cops to the revered president of the University of California.

The size of this fiscal iceberg is still unknown but it's huge. Maybe it's big enough to sink the state, much like the pension extravagance that helped push New York into bankruptcy in the 1970s. The CHP disability-pension scam is just the $15.5-million tip of the iceberg. That's how much money the state will squeeze from its law-abiding citizens this year to pay for the explosion in CHP disability pension costs.

The system is so generous that only one in four CHP officers retires on an ordinary service pension. Seventy-five percent go out on disability. Many of them are able-bodied officers complaining of a variety of vague aches and pains, physical and emotional—backed up by a diagnosis provided by doctors who specialize in winning disability pensions, instead of treating disabilities.

Everyone—the cop on the street and the bookkeepers in the Capitol, the "whore doctors" who feed on the system and the legislators who wink at it— knows the disability-pension system is filled with fraud and fueled by lies. In this year of huge state-budget deficits, some of these insiders are grumbling, but no one is willing to speak out.

"Hey," we say. "Some of these guys aren't disabled!" The CHP, alas, is not alone.

What's going on? A scam so huge it takes your breath away—but the CHP is not alone. Police officers up and down California—and across the nation—have been working the pension angle for decades. They can go out on disability even when they can run a marathon.

In Denver, Police Chief Ari Zavaras didn't go that far. He just went out on the links. At his retirement party, the chief said he planned to play a lot of golf. A week later, after a newspaper reported he was getting a tax-free disability pension, Zavaras was complaining about a bad back he traced to a misstep getting off a motorcycle twenty-three years earlier.

"Sometimes," the golfing chief said, "it's all I can do to get around." Sure.

Meanwhile, in California, "public servants"—many of them highly paid bureaucrats—have been getting inflated pensions through something known in the business as "spiking." Their salaries mysteriously shoot upward as they near retirement. That, in turn, "spikes" their pensions—and drives a spike into the personal budgets of the people who pay the taxes.

More exalted state employees don't have to stoop that low to reach so high. They simply leave with huge but entirely legal pension packages—$2.5 million for UC President David Gardner.

How CHP Officers Bilk Us— "Whore Doctors" Make It Easy

For a CHP officer, the disability-pension process often begins not with an injury, but with a visit to a "whore doctor." A whore doctor is a physician who sells services with no questions asked.

"They're not hard to find. The union newspapers run ads for lawyers who specialize in worker-comp cases," says one highway patrolman. "They'll send you to a whore doctor."

An officer doesn't have to worry about any time-consuming examinations or painful tests from a whore doctor. This fellow isn't in business to treat sick people. He's here to grind out medical reports. He hands his new patient a shopping list of disabilities. The officer picks out a plausible ailment and walks out with a report that guarantees a disability pension.

"A state doctor will look at it," says a CHP officer familiar with the system, "but he won't challenge it. He doesn't want to send somebody out on the street and then have him get injured—and wind up getting sued for malpractice."

Few "disabled" officers retire because of gunshot wounds or major injuries. Most go out complaining about a bad back or legs or neck, or maybe emotional burnout—"things that are hard to diagnose," as one expert describes the typical disability injuries.

Retire Early, Get More Money

The average Highway Patrol officer who retires on disability is in his forties—ten years younger than officers who keep on working and retire on a normal pension. He gets a bigger pension, and it's tax-free.

Already 69 percent of all retired CHP officers—2,548 out of 3,719—are on disability, and it's likely to get worse. In the last three years, an average of 73 percent of retiring officers applied for disability pensions; last year, the number was 81 percent.

These aren't abstract figures. They hit taxpayers in the family budget. Disability pensions are bigger, and since "disabled" officers retire early they will collect pensions longer—don't count on their "disabilities" to shorten their life spans. On top of all that, disability pensions are tax-free.

This year, the spectacular rate of disability pensions left the CHP budget $15.5 million short. The CHP had to ask the legislature for extra money to pay the bill.

"Isn't there something strange," a reporter asked a CHP spokesman," about how these guys all just magically become disabled when they're ready to retire? One day they're out on the street; the next day they're disabled."

The spokesman approached the question cautiously but with more candor than the ordinary bureaucrat. "The thinking is," he said, "I'll make a request. Maybe I'll get it. I've nothing to lose, and if I get it, I get a bigger pension."

Take the case of two Highway Patrol officers who each earn $3,670 a month, top pay for a state traffic officer. One of them works twenty-two years and retires on a regular pension. He gets $1,617 a month—44 percent of his salary—in a taxable pension. The other works seventeen years and goes out on disability. He gets $1,838 a month—50 percent of his salary—in a tax-free pension.

Retire five years earlier, get $221 a month more, and forget about the taxes—it's amazing that the disability-retirement rate hasn't hit 100 percent.

Everyone Does It

In Washington, D.C., the rate came close to doing just that. In the late 1960s, 95 percent of the retiring firefighters and police officers in the nation's capital were leaving with disability pensions. The minimum age for normal retirement was fifty—young by ordinary standards but too old for these guardians of law and order.

Then, beginning in 1970, Washington's police and fire departments saw a dramatic improvement in the health of their employees. The disability-retirement rate was cut nearly in half.

What caused the remarkable recovery? A new law that abolished the age requirement and tightened disability rules. Now firefighters and police officers didn't have to wait until the ripe old age of fifty. They could retire any time after twenty years of service. So they took an ordinary pension and skipped the tougher disability hearings.

New York City had a similar experience. With a minimum retirement age of fifty-five, seven out of ten retired early on disability. When the minimum age disappeared, the city's cops' health improved dramatically. The 70 percent disability rate dropped to 10 percent.

The pattern is the same across the country: raise the normal retirement age, and officers beat the system by retiring early on disability. Lower the retirement age, and the health of police officers magically improves. Disability pensions decrease.

A National Scandal by Any Standard

In a 1984 book, Dan McGill, an expert on pensions, was quoted as calling the police and fire disability-pension system as "almost a national scandal."

This year, McGill was reminded of the quote. He thought for a few seconds, then decided to drop the "almost."

"It is a national scandal," McGill said emphatically.

"The public-employee pension plans tend to be quite generous," said McGill, the founding director of the Pension Research Council at the prestigious Wharton School in Philadelphia. "And the system is administered in a sympathetic fashion. Disability is a very lucrative benefit. Usually the disability benefits are tax-exempt, and often there is a higher level of benefits than ordinary pensions."

What sorts of "disabilities" are most common, a reporter asked McGill—bad backs, that sort of thing?

"Yes," McGill said, "things that can't be diagnosed."

And with police-pension boards often filled with police officers, he said, the "disabled" officer gets a sympathetic hearing—and early retirement with a big pension.

"There's every motivation to get disability. It almost gets to be routine."

When it comes to the California Highway Patrol, you can drop the "almost." With 81 percent of CHP officers applying for disability pensions, these pensions have become truly routine.

New York City added its own wrinkle to the ugly picture of pension abuse after the state legislature passed the "heart bill" in the 1960s. The bill said that any heart disease suffered by a police officer or firefighter should be considered service-related and qualify the officer for an "accidental-disability" pension.

Hearts began beating wildly as officers learned that one of these disability pensions would pay them 75 percent of their regular salaries, far above the 50 percent they'd get with an ordinary service pension. Quickly, a tidal wave of cardiac disease swept through the uniformed ranks.

Actuaries had expected thirty officers to retire on accidental disability. Instead, 740 took advantage of it. At the same time, the number of ordinary retirements dropped by about two-thirds—486 instead of the expected 1,542.

The heart epidemic helped swamp New York City. The city was barely treading water fiscally as pension costs rose at a rate of 12 percent a year in the 1960s and 1970s.

By 1975, the city had $3 billion of unpaid bills and no money to pay them. For years, the big banks had been lending to the city at rates more commonly charged by loan sharks. Now they refused to make loans at any price, and the state finally took control of the city's financial affairs.

One financial analyst who sifted through the debris concluded that the cause of the disaster was simple. "The city," he said, "lived beyond its means." And one of the main reasons was the lavish pension system, topped off by the extraordinary "heart bill."

And New York's taxpayers wound up paying the bill.

The Choice: Be a Liar or a Fool

For an officer who wants to retire honestly, the pension system can be as frustrating and infuriating as his work on the streets in Los Angeles.

"I'm forty," the officer says. "I'll have twenty years in next year. I want to retire. I love the job. I'm a company man. I like the department. It's been good to me, but I've got kids now. It's a dangerous job and I've got other things I want to do."

The officer called to check up on how to retire at forty-one. The answer was simple: he couldn't—unless he lied.

"You have to be fifty years old with twenty years' service to retire," he says. "They said, if I retire next year, they'll treat it like a resignation. I've got twenty years but I won't get a pension until I'm fifty."

But the man on the other end of the phone told the officer that there was another way out: "He said, 'You can take a disability pension. I've got your record here. You can qualify.'

"He doesn't approve of it," the officer says, "but he said most people will take it. I could qualify. I have been injured over the years. I have some hearing loss from riding a motorcycle. I have legitimate headaches from an accident. I could get disability."

There's only one problem: the officer isn't disabled. He's still working, still riding a motorcycle, still getting a rush of excitement from a chase, still enjoying his work, still doing a good job. He's got aches and pains but he's not disabled. After twenty years, he feels he deserves a pension, but the only way he can get it is by claiming to be disabled.

"They encourage dishonesty," the officer says. "On the street you consistently see miscarriages of justice. Nobody goes to jail. They get off and back out on the street. You see so much graft and corruption all around and you wonder why not do it? Why not go out on disability?"

Why doesn't he do it?

"I don't want to lie about it," he says firmly. Then, thinking wistfully about all those officers who do lie, he ends on a uncertain note: "Still, I don't want to be a fool."

The Honest Cop and the Crooked Doc

Highway Patrol officers call them "whore doctors"—physicians who do whatever you want. For a price.

The whore doctors specialize in workers'-compensation and disability-retirement scams. If you want to collect, you go to the doctor. He gives you a list of likely ailments. You pick out your favorite, and he writes up a diagnosis that fits the bill.

The process works smoothly—unless you happen to really be sick. Whore doctors aren't accustomed to dealing with sick people. They're so used to faking a diagnosis, they don't recognize a real illness when they see it.

That's what happened to one Highway Patrol officer who was injured while working a motorcycle patrol a few years ago.

"I went down hard, got hurt big time," the officer recalls. "I didn't have my own doctor, so I asked a friend. He sent me to a lawyer who recommended one. I went to her, and she took five hundred pieces of data from me—my age, weight, height, where the accident happened—five hundred things. Then she fed it into a computer, hit a button, and out came twenty different medical reports. I could have my pick."

That was all he got—no treatment for his aching head, just a table filled with medical reports. All he had to do was pick one and get his money—as much as a year's "4800 time," followed by a disability pension. The "4800 time," named after section 4800 of the state labor code, would give him full pay, tax-free, while he stayed at home and waited to retire.

Oh, the officer did get one more thing from the doctor: "a wink and a nod." She never said that the session was a farce—she was to smooth for that—but she couldn't keep from grinning.

"I told her that I was really hurting," the officer says. "She just said, 'Sure you are,' and gave me a wink and a nod."

The officer went back to the lawyer to complain. The lawyer misunderstood. "I'll get you another doctor," he said.

"Not one like her," the officer said. "I'm really hurt."

"You're really hurt?" the lawyer asked in astonishment.

"Yeah."

"Why didn't you say so?" the lawyer asked, without a trace of irony.

He found a real doctor for the officer, and a few hours later, the officer was admitted to the hospital for treatment of a serious head injury.

Only One Sure Cure for This Epidemic of Greed

A CHP spokesman says the Highway Patrol can control the epidemic itself. An outside expert thinks it may be an incurable disease. We think they're both wrong.

The CHP's remedy is a new disability-fraud unit designed to catch the fakers, says Sam Haynes, a Highway Patrol spokesman. "The commissioner's concerned about the high rate of disability retirement," Haynes says. "That's why he set up the unit."

The unit's job is complicated, though, by a state law that requires Highway Patrol officers to be able to perform the whole range of duties of a traffic officer. That prevents the CHP from putting partially disabled officers on "light duty," Haynes says.

Others within the CHP think the epidemic can be controlled by changing the law. "Get rid of the silly rule that, if you're not a hundred percent available for duty, you have to retire," one officer says. "There are sixteen tasks. If you can't perform one of them, you can't be a CHP officer. Why not have limited-duty jobs—working as permanent field officers or reviewing accident reports. Maybe you'll get better and go back out."

Dan McGill, a man who has spent his life studying public pensions, is less optimistic. McGill talked about the problem in a phone conversation from his office at Wharton, the famed business school in Philadelphia.

"Is there any solution to these pension scams?" a reporter asked. Even over the phone, he could sense that McGill was shrugging his shoulders in despair as he answered.

"I don't know of any," McGill said. "It's a political thing and they're always organized

Already 59% Disabled*

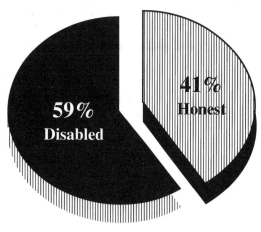

59%
Disabled

41%
Honest

*Percentage of all retired CHP officers
(2,548 out of 3,719) currently on disability

And Getting Worse

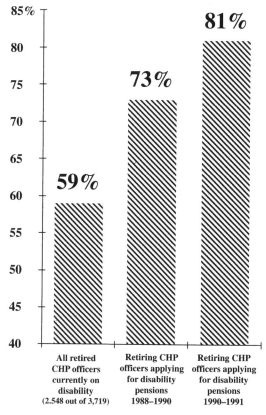

59%

73%

81%

| All retired CHP officers currently on disability (2,548 out of 3,719) | Retiring CHP officers applying for disability pensions 1988–1990 | Retiring CHP officers applying for disability pensions 1990–1991 |

CALIFORNIA HIGHWAY PATROL MONTHLY PENSIONS
Honest vs. Disabled Cops

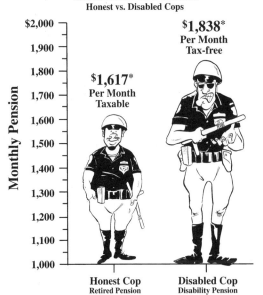

$1,617*
Per Month
Taxable

$1,838*
Per Month
Tax-free

Monthly Pension

Honest Cop
Retired Pension

Disabled Cop
Disability Pension

*Based on a monthly salary of $3,670 per month (top pay for state traffic officers).

into unions. Exposure is the only thing—like what you're doing. When they're exposed, there's some tidying up done—until people forget about it."

McGill may well be correct. But that doesn't mean that the public must continue to submit to these fleecings by public-pension funds that are supported by our taxes.

The solution to the disability disease is radical surgery: cut out public pensions entirely.

Even the good guys on the public payroll become obsessed with their pensions. They spend more time talking about what they'll do after retirement than about what they're doing right now. We ought to make sure that they are obsessed with their work. The best way to do that is to pay them what they're worth for what they're doing now.

Instead of dreaming of early retirement, they ought to be thinking about how to do a better job and make more money here and now. Let them set aside part of that pay for their own retirement.

This isn't an original idea. Some of America's Founding Fathers wanted the Constitution to include a ban on pensions for civil servants. They had seen how the British had abused the public-pension system, and they wanted to spare the new nation from an Old World corruption.

Those enlightened fellows lost the battle two hundred years ago. Now we're paying the price.

TO DO

BAGATORIALS

IS GLORIOUS

To Read Is Good

Children Who Love to Read Go Farther

Your mind is a muscle, said a very smart man.[1] It ought to be trained and exercised. We live in a difficult world. We must be clever to be able to do the decent thing and to prosper at the same time. To be clever, to be happy, we have to be able to deal with more than just the nuts and bolts of existence. We must be able to use ideas, to be creative, and to imagine. To learn to imagine, happy children read.

Reading is still the best known method for children to develop their imaginations. Television and movies are terrific, easy, and fun, but never as good as a well-loved book.

A good book opens doors into fabulous worlds. It entertains. A local library has thousands of possibilities. Best of all, when the book is finished and returned, the mind keeps thinking. A book that makes a child curious expands the child's own universe—along paths chosen by the child. The ability to turn letters into words and words into thoughts is magic. Learning stories is the root of intelligence.

Reading must be learned, but you can make learning fun and easy. Lucky is the child who learns to read by being read to. It's fun to spend time with a child. If you pick the books both enjoy, both love the time together. The earlier you start to read to a child, the sooner the child learns to read on his own. Reading to your child is the same as building a foundation for a house. Reading, writing, and speaking skills will all be built on the child's urge to learn to know what's in a book.

Choose children's books carefully. You're going to want them to read books which interest them. You'll want the books to inspire a child to do the decent thing. Take the story of *Mike Mulligan and His Steam Shovel*:[2] an exciting, heroic story about heavy equipment and hard work. It's good for both parent and child! You can find books about trains, trucks, animals, jobs, cartoon

Encourage young readers by paying them to read.

characters— anything you like. Better yet, let the child choose with your help. The point is to read together, and both be interested.

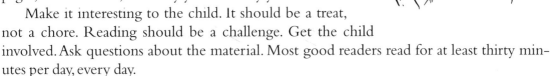

Set aside some time for reading every day. Turn off the television and the radio, and go to a quiet place so you can relax and read with undivided attention. Most people read books, but almost anything will do, including comic books, the sports pages, baseball cards, or a story you wrote by yourself.

Make it interesting to the child. It should be a treat, not a chore. Reading should be a challenge. Get the child involved. Ask questions about the material. Most good readers read for at least thirty minutes per day, every day.

Relate the reading to your child's activities. If your child is learning about numbers, colors, or the alphabet, read all about them in a book. If your child loves fire engines, read a book about fire engines, and then visit the fire station. Reading will inform and explain. Soon, your child will be an expert on the subject!

As your child grows, you will find yourself reading some favorite books over and over. Kids have an uncanny ability to memorize. Your child will be able to "read" some books back to you just by reciting the story from memory. When your children pick out the words on paper that go with the spoken word, then they're well on the way to reading on their own.

Keep track of the books you read together, so your child can take pride in the accomplishment. Some families put a list on the refrigerator. Others use a poster or a reading tree. We know parents who give gold stars for books read. We know families who discuss children's books at the dinner table. Reading books can become a favorite game and activity. Praise your child for reading.

Get a library card for every child, and use it weekly. Most libraries have a story time for toddlers. Try to fit it in your schedule, because your child will love it. Then, select some books to check out. Library cards are easy to get and fun to use.

When you read aloud, be happy. Some people are self-conscious about making mistakes when they read, but mistakes happen. Go back and say it correctly. This shows your child it is natural to stumble on words. Learning can be frustrating, so encourage your child to try, try again. Praise your child when your child reads well and encourage your child to recover when your child falters.

Fathers especially ought to set an example of reading. Seventy percent of the pupils in remedial reading classes are boys. Set an example. In fifteen years, you'll have plenty of time to watch TV, talk to friends, and go shopping, but your child may have lost the opportunity to learn to love to read from you.

On the other hand, as good teachers say, "Every child has his own appointment with learning." Be patient and it will come. Keep reading stories, especially stories that are fabulous and fanciful, because the ability to create an image in the mind is the same skill children use later to learn and handle abstract thoughts such as algebra.

But what about parents? You'd do well to read a daily newspaper and talk about it to someone. "Never have I found myself in such difficulty, that I could not regain my composure with some time spent reading," wrote Montesquieu. There's a magazine to help you in your trade. There's an author who will tickle your fancy and brighten your life. Good luck!

A Few of Our Favorite Books

0–18 Months

Animals, and little books read over and over again are perfect for the littlest readers. Here are some suggestions:
Goodnight Moon, Margaret Wise Brown
Alphabet, Fiona Pragoff
Jamberry, Bruce Degen
Moo Moo, Peekaboo!, Jane Dyer
Little Duck, Peggy Tagel
Pat the Cat, Edith Kunharot

18–36 Months

Use books to learn concepts like shapes, colors, and textures. Pop-up books are big favorites.
Freight Train, D. Crews
How Many Bugs in a Box?, David A. Carter
Brown Bear, Brown Bear, What Do You See?, Eric Carle
Make Way for Ducklings, Robert McCloskey
The Tale of Peter Rabbit, Beatrix Potter
The Very Hungry Caterpillar, Eric Carle

3–5 Years

This age group likes to snuggle and hear simple, comforting stories. They like to take a book they've heard a million times and "read" it back to you. Children 4–6 are interested in silliness, nonsense, and rhymes. They also like books with more intricate illustrations such as those by Maurice Sendak.
Curious George, H. A. Rey
Where the Wild Things Are, Maurice Sendak
Green Eggs and Ham, and *The Cat in the Hat*, Dr. Seuss
Corduroy books, Don Freeman
King Bidgood's in the Bathtub, Audrey Wood
The Story of Babar, the Little Elephant, Jean de Brunhoff

6–8 Years

Cloudy with a Chance of Meatballs, Judi Barrett
A Bear Called Paddington, Michael Bond
The Secret Life of Walter Mitty, James Thurber
The Twelve Dancing Princesses, Marianna Mayer
The Velveteen Rabbit, Margery Williams
Madeline, Ludwig Bemelmans

Alexander and the Terrible, Horrible, No Good, Very Bad Day, Judith Viorst
The Jolly Postman, Janet and Allan Ahlberg
James and the Giant Peach, Roald Dahl
Charlotte's Web, E. B. White

8–10 Years
Charlie and the Chocolate Factory and *Fantastic Mr. Fox,* Roald Dahl
Mrs. Piggle-Wiggle books, Betty MacDonald
Encyclopedia Brown books, Donald Sobol
Winnie the Pooh, A. A. Milne
Little House series, Laura Ingalls Wilder
The Secret Garden, Frances Hodgson Burnett
Where the Sidewalk Ends, Shel Silverstein

10–12 Years
Alice's Adventures in Wonderland, Lewis Carroll
The Borrowers, Mary Norton
The Cricket in Times Square, George Selden
Pippi Longstocking, Astrid Lindgren
Sounder, William H. Armstrong
Harriet the Spy, Louise Fitzhugh
Just So Storiers, Rudyard Kipling
The Lion, the Witch and the Wardrobe, C. S. Lewis
Where the Red Fern Grows, Wilson Rawls
The Twenty-one Balloons, William Pène du Bois
The Great Brain, John D. Fitzgerald
The Phantom Tollbooth, Norton Justen (this is the best!)
Mrs. Frisby and the Rats of NIMH, Robert C. O'Brien

12 and Up
To Kill a Mockingbird, Harper Lee
Treasure Island, Robert Louis Stevenson
The Diary of Anne Frank, Anne Frank
All Creatures Great and Small, James Herriot
Little Women, Louise May Alcott
Scary Stories to Tell in the Dark, Alvin Schwartz
The Egypt Game, Zilpha Keatley Snyder
The Hobbit, J. R. R. Tolkien
Julie of the Wolves, Jean Craighead George
The Witch of Blackbird Pond, Elizabeth George Speare
A Wrinkle in Time, Madeleine L'Engle

The Customer Company employees are encouraged to read books in several ways. Reading six books a year, including at least three fiction books, is one of the requirements of our 1-percent bonus plan. We pay five dollars per book, and we pay for the book, for any employee who reads a book off our company reading list. We learn about

> The reading of all good books is indeed like a conversation with the noblest men of past centuries who were the authors of them, nay a carefully studied conversation, in which they reveal to us none but the best of their thoughts.
>
> —*René Descartes,* Discourse on Method, 1
>
> " 'Tis the good reader that makes the good book; . . . in every book he finds passages which seem confidences or asides hidden from all else and unmistakably meant for his ear; the profit of books is according to the sensibility of the reader; the profoundest thought or passion sleeps as in a mine, until it is discovered by an equal mind and heart."
>
> —*Ralph Waldo Emerson, "Success," a chapter in* Society and Solitude *(1870).*

new books from book reviews in *The New York Times, The Wall Street Journal,* and the Sunday newspaper, which we sell at a discounted price in all eighty Cheaper! stores in Northern and Central California. If you know someone looking for a good retail job, ask him or her to talk to one of our managers!

[1]Jack LaLanne, the exercise expert. Later attributed to Carl Sagan.
[2]Virginia Lee Burton wrote *Mike Mulligan and His Steam Shovel.*

Read to Get Rich!

Only 1 percent of Americans read more than one book last year.

Less than half read a daily newspaper. Only a small percentage read magazines. If you're reading this, you're already one of the elite.

Reading helps us understand the world. It's part of a happy and productive life. Reading helps to free us from the tyranny of others. Most of us are raised and educated to fit a certain mindset. We need information and knowledge to question our own logic, to build our own philosophy, free from the restrictions of others. People must choose how to run their own lives. Living this life is easier if your philosophy is based on a logical, realistic, and informed view of the world. Reading gets you there.

Reading can also be very enjoyable. It can be enormously entertaining. It allows us to expand our horizons beyond our present situation. Once you start to read, you'll keep reading.

You can persuade your children to read by starting to read by yourself. Discuss books with your children. Make books and magazines available to them. Read to them when they are young, then pay them to read by themselves.

We pay our employees to read because we've found it's better to do business with people who think. We have a reading list of our favorite books. If employees read a book on the list, we reimburse them for the cost of the book and send them a $5 gift certificate.

We'll make the same offer to you for a very special book: *Atlas Shrugged* by Ayn Rand. *Atlas Shrugged* is one of the most important books of our time. It was written in 1957 by Ayn Rand, who emigrated to the United States from Russia. This exciting novel pits individualists against the corrosive force of authority. *Time* magazine originally reviewed it as a work of science fiction, but events have shown that even Ayn Rand underestimated the damage inflicted by statists. This is a book for all ages. It tells you that you are the most important person in the world and you can and should take charge of your own life.

Books We Recommend

Here are some of the books we recommend. Everybody's list is specific to what he or she does. This list has helped us run better stores. We'd like to see your list.

You might want to start with a book about books. We suggest *How to Read a Book: The Classic Guide to Intelligent Reading.*

Mortimer Adler wrote the first edition of this book in 1940 and rewrote it with Charles Van Doren in 1972. *The New Yorker* said this book is "a rare phenomenon, a living classic. It is the best and most successful guide to reading comprehension for the general reader."

There's more to the world than you see on the nightly news. If you want broader horizons or a deeper understanding of why things happen, you ought to read a publication of

international quality. We recommend you subscribe to *The Wall Street Journal, The Economist, Forbes,* or *Business Week.*

These publications are so valuable that we reimburse our employees for 50 percent of the cost of a subscription. Over the years, *The Wall Street Journal* has been a tremendous source of news and argument. It favors freedom. *The Economist,* from London, has an international view that will shock and surprise you.

Some of the other books on our reading list include:

TITLE	AUTHOR	PUBLISHER	COMMENTS
Main Street Merchant	J.C. Penney	Out of print	the best
The One Minute Manager	Blanchard and Johnson	Morrow	good, fast, but trite
The Effective Executive	Peter Drucker	Harper & Row	a classic
How to Stop Smoking Permanently	Walter S. Ross	Little, Brown & Co.	may save your life

TITLE	AUTHOR	PUBLISHER	COMMENTS
The Goal	Eli Goldratt	North River Press	very useful
The Incredible Bread Machine	Brown, Keating, et al	World Research	fundamental
Dress for Success	John Molloy	Warner	yes, it matters
Managing	Harold Geneen	Doubleday	"managers must manage"
Think and Grow Rich	Napoleon Hill	Fawcett	could happen to you
How I Found Freedom in an Unfree World	Harry Browne	Avon	entertaining and obvious
Selling It Like It Is	David Ogilvy	Crown Publishing	by the master
The Economics and Politics of Race	Thomas Sowell	Morrow	there's a reason
Keep On Going	Les Schwab	Schwab	tire man does good
In Pursuit of Happiness	Charles Murray	Simon & Schuster	think about it
De-Managing America	Richard Cornuelle	Vintage	sensible
Good to Eat	Marvin Harris	Simon & Schuster	why you eat what

A Romantic Dinner

What to Do When You're Invited

When someone invites you to a romantic dinner, respond quickly. Tell your hostess* "yes" or "no," or "I'll get back to you," but you must say something. If you tell her you will get back to her, then make sure you do!

If you want to go, nail down the particulars. When? Where? Can you bring something? Your hostess probably will tell you she has everything, but it's polite to ask. Make a note of the date and time, so you can make sure you show up on time. Plan what you'll wear. Try to make a good impression. Romance comes from showing your best. Neat, clean, and presentable make an evening more pleasant.

Be Prepared!

The secret of a true romantic evening is to put as much effort into being a good guest as your hostess puts into being a good hostess. Even if your hostess has everything, bring a token of your appreciation. Buy a bottle of fine wine or a bouquet of flowers. Make it a pleasant surprise for your hostess. Spend time preparing for the dinner. Make up a list of at least seven topics. Think about what you'll say. If you're prepared, you'll be more at ease.

Some of our favorite topics include:

Where do you really want to go in all the world? Where would you go for the vacation of your dreams?

Who was your best friend when you were a child? What ever became of that person?

When was the best day you ever had in your entire life? Why was it so good?

Where was the best meal you ever ate? Why was it so good? What did you eat?

*We decided, arbitrarily, to talk about a male guest and a female hostess, for ease of writing, but of course the roles are often reversed.

What are you going to be when you grow up? What do you want to do someday? How are you going to get there?

When You Arrive

Be punctual! A romantic dinner takes a lot of work. You should show up on time to make it easier. Why make the hostess worry? If the home looks special, or the table is nicely set, mention it to your hostess. If your hostess is beautiful, say so! Offer your token of appreciation at the door, and express your gratitude for the invitation right from the get-go.

At dinner, relax and enjoy it. Look for all the good things your hostess has prepared for you. Mention them. Compliment your hostess. How is the food? Find something positive to say, and keep the conversation going. This is when you make a contribution by being appreciative and charming. If the food is delicious, let her know!

OK, so you're wondering, what if your feelings for the other person are different from her feelings for you? What if the feeling isn't mutual? It happens all the time. Be gracious about it. Be a good person, but you must be candid at the same time. Unrequited love is horrible, but it's even worse to be led on about it. Instead, be yourself and be friendly. Who knows when you'll need a very good friend? Above all, in this situation, avoid the worst faux pas of all. If at the end you say, "Let's just be friends," any horrible thing your hostess does to you is justified.

Whatever the outcome, after dinner, make sure you express your gratitude. You'd be surprised how many people forget to say how much they appreciate the efforts of others. Well, here's your chance. Be a gentleman.

Send a note of thanks during the next week. Think about how you can reciprocate. Make sure your hostess knows her efforts were worthwhile. . . .

Etiquette Helps

The purpose of etiquette is to help people feel better, live better, and relate to each other more easily, says Letitia Baldrige in the introduction to the classic *The Amy Vanderbilt Complete Book of Etiquette.** Mrs. Baldrige writes:

> My philosophy of manners is that they were based on efficiency, yes, but even more on a superb trait of character called kindness. "Etiquette" is a starchy word, but manners are not starchy. . . . Real manners are being thoughtful toward others' problems. There is nothing formal or stiff about that!

*Published by Doubleday. It's in libraries and bookstores everywhere.

Having good manners gives one a feeling of security in dealing with people. . . . This book
is an exercise in options. Because fortunately the hidebound rules of behavior have relaxed. . . .
What has not changed is the need for consideration of others. . . . My goal: to help people
make it through life just a little more easily and be a little more sure of themselves.

A book on etiquette can help you learn how to be graceful and knowledgeable. Think
of it as a reservoir of years of experience, ready for you to use to make your life and the lives
of those around you more pleasant.

How to Prepare and Serve a Romantic Dinner— a Simple, Gracious, Special Meal

Why does romance bloom? Often because somebody takes the time to be nice. A pleasant, well-planned dinner is an accomplishment. A truly romantic dinner is an artistic
achievement of the highest order. Simple or extravagant, the better you plan it, the more
likely you are to create a special moment.

First, remember timing is everything. When is the best day to serve your dinner? At what
time? (We assume you've already selected your guest.) An easy night when you can finish the
work and relax enough to enjoy the evening is best. If you have kids, arrange a baby-sitter.
Pick a time when the baby will be asleep. You'll need time before the dinner to prepare and
to calm down. Time free from interruption helps to make your dinner go smoothly.

Invite your guest at least a week ahead of time, even if it's your spouse. Call him on the
phone or write an invitation. Tell him when you would like him to arrive. Both of you
should look forward to the dinner. Wouldn't it be awful to go to all the trouble only to discover your guest has other plans?

Make your shopping list early. There's one on the side of this bag. Don't forget the napkins, tablecloth (or placemats), and candles. Add a bunch of fresh flowers to your decora-
tions.

Go through the meal several times. Do you have croutons and dressing for the salad? Napkins? Butter and sour cream for the potatoes? A little touch, such as whipped cream on the ice
cream, can show you planned ahead.

Clean your home before you start your final preparations, even if it means throwing
everything in another room. You're setting the stage. Your guest should notice a transforma-
tion in the room.

Prepare what you can as early as you can. Put a damp paper towel over the salad in the
refrigerator to keep the lettuce crisp even though you made it in the early afternoon. Scrub
the potatoes for baking long before you need them. Don't forget to chill the wine!

Decide what to wear several days in advance. You'll want to make sure it's clean and it fits. Think about what you'll discuss. Remember, your guest may be nervous, or maybe even a little put off by all your preparations, so you'll want to think of ways to put him at ease. What music will be best? How will you serve the drinks? Walk through it a couple of times to make sure you'll be knowledgeable and calm.

Put the potatoes in the oven at 375 degrees an hour before you plan to serve dinner. Be ready for your guest fifteen minutes before the anticipated time. While you wait, you can set out the chips and salsa, or prepare the pot stickers for steaming. Relax and enjoy your preparations.

Here's the important part: No matter how difficult it's been, when your guest arrives, greet him with a smile. Offer him a drink, and point out the hors d'oeuvres. Start making small talk while you heat the grill. Both the steaks and the chicken take only a few minutes to cook, so, when you are about ready, season the entrée with salt and pepper and grill them according to the directions on the side panel, which you've memorized. Now it's time to fix the noodles. Put the rolls in the oven to warm after you turn the steaks over. Pull potatoes and rolls out of the oven, add dressing to your salad, and put a steak and potato on each plate. Serve the butter, the sour cream, the salad, and the rolls at the table.

When you light the candles, the ceremony begins. You've turned off the TV. Maybe you've even unplugged the telephone. Set your guest at ease. It's time to let it happen. Enjoy yourself.

Expect the unexpected. If the steaks burn, if catastrophe strikes, smile and laugh. You can go to Plan B. Your guest already knows you've gone to great lengths to make the evening special. Few people take the time to make a romantic dinner. Just the attempt is a treat in and of itself. Practice makes perfect!

Here's What an Expert Says About Table Setting

No matter how simple the meal, it's nice to have the table properly set. Knives, then spoons should be on the right side of each place setting, forks on the left. The easiest rule is to place the utensils in the order of their use during the particular meal, starting at the outside. This setting is for a dinner that begins with soup, followed by a main course (large knife and fork), salad (small fork), and dessert; the butter and/or cheese knife goes to the right of the big knife. If you were having salad as a first course, the two forks would be reversed and no soup spoon would be needed.

These rules assume you have plenty of silver. If you haven't, don't worry. Don't hesitate to serve more than just one course because of lack of tableware. You can slip out between courses and wash up whatever is needed or simply ask guests to keep a knife or a fork.

Napkins go to the left of the forks or under them. Or you can do something fancy, like making the napkin into a fan shape and putting it in the middle of each place setting or stuffing it into a large goblet. Glasses for wine and water are always to the right of the setting. If you are serving both red and white wine, put the smaller glass for white on the outside. Butter plates, when used, are to the left.

Most important, whether for guests or when you're just family, remember to warm your plates and serving bowls and platters whenever you serve hot food. Warm everything in a low oven or on the back of the stove, if you have room; if not, a radiator, a hot plate, and the drying cycle of a dishwasher makes excellent plate warmers.*

Use your best dishes. Remember the wine glasses, the water glasses, and the salt & pepper! Even if you plan to cook to perfection, your guest might ask for it. Will your guest want sugar in his coffee? Milk or cream? Be prepared for the possibilities.

*excerpted from the *Fannie Farmer Cookbook,* by Marion Cunningham, which is super.

Deciding What to Serve

Choose a meal you're confident you can cook easily. The food is only part of your concerns! We suggest:

A Great Dinner	A Superb Dinner
Appetizers:	*Appetizers:*
It'sa Chips and Salsa	pot stickers
Wine:	*Wine:*
Round Hill Cabernet	White Zinfandel
Entrée:	*Entrée:*
broiled steaks green salad baked potatoes	sautéed chicken breasts over buttered noodles
Dessert:	green salad garlic bread
ice cream and chocolate sauce	*Dessert:*
and for after dinner:	sliced peaches over ice cream
Cooks Extra Dry Champagne	*and for after dinner:*
	Champagne

Shopping List

It'sa Tortilla Chips 16 oz. (freshly made with Canola oil)	Split chicken breasts 4 lb.	garlic bread	chocolate sauce
		potatoes	whipped cream
	New York Strip	noodles	Sutter Home Zinfandel
Pot stickers 40 oz. (hot sauce included in bag!)	Steak—Choice	butter	Round Hill Cabernet
	lettuce	sour cream	Cooks Champagne
	salad dressing	peaches (canned)	Freixenet Champagne
	salsa	ice cream	coffee

Words of Praise
for Good Manners

"Manners are the happy ways of doing things."

▼

By the time you read this bag, your manners may be set in stone. There is a way you do things, a way you treat other people, a way you handle each situation, and those ways are your manners. If you act with courtesy and kindness, people say you have good manners. If you're rude, ill-mannered, and selfish, then you have poor manners. Manners are habits. They're hard to learn and hard to break. If you can make the effort to improve your manners, you can become happier, healthier, and wealthier.

We'd be happier if we followed these simple rules:

- Act toward others as you want them to act toward you.
- Say "please" and "thank you."
- Let others speak until they are finished. Let people finish their own sentences.
- If someone is on the telephone, wait for him to finish before speaking to him.

THE MANNERS MACHINE

MAN Ⓐ HOLDS OPEN DOOR Ⓑ FOR WOMAN Ⓒ, REVEALING CLOCK Ⓓ. WOMAN, NOT WANTING TO KEEP FRIENDS WAITING, HURRIES ONTO TREADMILL Ⓔ, PULLING ROPE Ⓕ THROUGH PULLEY Ⓖ, AND RAISING ELBOWS Ⓗ OFF TABLE Ⓘ. RISING FORK Ⓙ POPS BALLOON Ⓚ, LITTERING FLOOR Ⓛ. MAN Ⓜ, HELPING OTHERS, SWEEPS GARBAGE INTO DUSTPAN Ⓝ, WEIGHING DOWN "ON" BUTTON Ⓞ, CAUSING TV Ⓟ TO FLASH GOLDEN RULE Ⓠ. VIEWER Ⓡ DECIDES TO GIVE UP SEAT Ⓢ, HITTING TARGET Ⓣ, LOWERING POLE Ⓤ, WHICH PULLS STRING Ⓥ, TURNING ON FAN Ⓦ, SENDING STREAMERS Ⓨ TO TICKLE MAN'S FANCY Ⓩ, AND CAUSING HIM TO SMILE.

- Smile at every opportunity.
- Introduce people to each other. Acknowledge people.
- Offer your seat to others if they stand while you sit. Offer to help others. Tip generously.
- If you hurt someone, try to help him. Apologize and learn from your mistake. Forgive those who hurt you.
- Keep your voice down. If someone yells at you, keep your cool.
- Be polite. Avoid foul language. Cussing is a weakness.
- Tell the truth and only the truth. Be nice or say nothing.
- Avoid gossip. Mind your own business.
- Cover your mouth. Say "excuse me" when you belch or make strange noises.
- Keep your elbows off the table. Sit up straight. Try to be graceful.
- Get permission before you borrow something.
- Hold the door open for the next person.
- If you open it, close it. If you break it, fix it. Think of others.
- Be punctual. Keep your promises.
- If you receive a gift, write a thank-you note that same day. If you're invited to something, respond within a week of getting the invitation, especially if it says "RSVP."
- Get to the point. People appreciate candor and brevity.

Trivial? George Washington carried a list of fifty-four manners to study and practice every day. Each and every day, Ben Franklin concentrated on one of thirteen virtues. Manners are virtues in action. Many great achievers think about John Wooden's Pyramid of Success every day. Manners are what you do. You show them in times of crisis and every hour of the day.

Americans use etiquette to "feel better, live better, and relate to each other more easily," writes Letitia Baldrige in the classic *Amy Vanderbilt Complete Book of Etiquette.* "My philosophy of manners is that they are based on efficiency, yes, but even more on a superb trait of character called kindness. . . . *Real manners* are being thoughtful toward others, being creative in doing nice things for others, or sympathizing with others' problems."[1]

Manners and etiquette are for everyday living. "We must all learn the socially acceptable ways of living with others in no matter what society we move."[2] Go to a bookstore and take a look at the etiquette books. Look at the table of contents. These books can help you to form a gracious personal style. It's an American tradition that good manners are good for everyone—and not just for formal dinner parties.

Manners are one of the longest, toughest lessons any young person learns. "Most young people think they are being natural when really they are just ill-mannered and crude," wrote La Rochefoucauld over three hundred years ago. Most young people learn by example. Want to teach your children something important? Be polite around them and to them. Children practice what they see. It's common sense. Decent people work at being well mannered. That grace leads to happiness.

The Joys of Dining:
Well-Mannered Family Dinners Are Good for All Ages

Happy families eat together. Eating together makes families happier when the cheerful ceremony of an evening meal puts the day into a satisfying order. It's more than food that makes a family meal so special. It's more than family itself. It's the way we act toward each other that turns mealtime into a happy time. Your manners make the difference.

Start with the ritual of getting together. It's good to see everybody all at one time. It's a relief when each member of the family contributes something to the table. Meals involve a lot of work in planning, shopping, cooking, setting the table, and cleaning up. Eating together makes the job more manageable when everybody helps out. Manners include doing your share of the work.

Manners also make the work of food preparation worth the effort. It's the kindness and appreciation that people show each other—for making the meal, for earning the wages that pay for the meal, for making life better for each other. Simple, inexpensive meals can be just as satisfying as large-scale productions. Enjoying each other is as important as enjoying the food, and to do that, we should be gracious and respectful.

A good dinner starts before the dinner. Someone announces the time for dinner and the family agrees to be there on time. Then the meal must be planned, purchased, and prepared. Get together before the meal, for a drink before dinner, so everybody has a chance to do their business, quench their thirst, wash their hands, and be ready for dinner. Manners include the way you make conversation. It's essential for you to share what's happening in each other's lives, graciously.

Commonsense Suggestions
- Eat at a table. Set it with care. Use napkins, forks, knives, spoons, salt, and pepper at every meal, so every meal is complete. Fresh flowers and dinner music add a nice touch. Use placemats or a tablecloth to make cleanup easier and to keep your table looking good.

- A regularly scheduled dinnertime makes planning easier. Announce the time well in advance.
- Be on time for dinner! Try to look your best. Take off your hat, wear a shirt, and wash your hands before you sit down.
- Put your napkin in your lap after you sit down. If you must leave during the meal, put it on the chair. When it comes time to leave, fold your napkin and leave it on the table. If you find yourself with a lot of forks, knives, and spoons, work from the outside in.
- Pass food to the left around the table. Make sure every dish goes to everyone. Wait until everyone is served before you begin eating.
- At a restaurant, if your tablemates are served before you, encourage them to start eating while the food is still hot.
- If you want something from across the table, ask someone to pass it. Reaching can cause a mess.
- Taste the food before you add salt and pepper, even at home. Chew with your mouth closed. Make an effort to be gracious. Swallow and empty your mouth before speaking. Sit up straight with your feet on the floor. Keep your elbows off the table, say some.
- Cut your food one piece at a time. Food is for eating and not for playing. Take small bites. Chew and swallow, then sip. Sips are better than gulps.
- When you are finished, rest your fork and knife together, fork up, on the right side of your plate. Stir your coffee or drink quietly.
- Wine makes the dinner special! It's important for children to see adults consume alcoholic beverages responsibly and in moderation.
- Make dinnertime a time without reading, television or telephone calls.
- Everyone should participate in the conversation. Start with "What happened to you today?" Every day, try to think of three new topics to talk about during dinner. Some must be coaxed into participation. Some will need to learn to get to the point!
- Mealtime is a happy time, but it's also a quiet time. It's not a time for singing or showing off. Make extra efforts to get along. If someone misbehaves or makes a mistake, be gracious but firm.
- If you must leave the table, ask to be excused. Compliment the cook on the dinner. Help clean up as much as you can.

Some days will be better than others. "Awkwardness at the dinner table is only increased by nagging. Children learn better table manners if they learn them slowly, and with a very clear edict to the older children in the family that no one is allowed to make fun of the younger one's errors,"[3] say the experts.

Besides making day after day nicer, well-mannered dinners prepare children to do well in life. "Poor table manners can be a serious deterrent to a student's social life at school and college, to anyone's career, and to a happy marriage. . . . Table manners are one of the most visible signals of the state of our manners."[4]

Top Topics for Happy Conversations

For many families, what's said is as important as what's eaten. They live to talk to each other. Letitia Baldrige writes: "In the give-and-take of this family situation, a child learns the art of conversation, a skill that will serve him all his life. He begins to learn what is of universal interest to all people; he feels the joy of wit when someone says something that makes everyone laugh. He hears his mother say, 'That's enough, Peter. That story has gone on far too long,' and he realizes why. He hears his father say, 'That was very well put, Suzanne,' and he begins to analyze why his sister earned that compliment."[5]

Good conversations are cheerful and informed. When a good conversation gets going, everybody has something to add and no one monopolizes the table. Conversations have ground rules in themselves, just as meals do. For instance, people learn to know when they've gone on too long. Or they learn when a topic has become overused. Some topics are, by mutual agreement, avoided at the table.

Some of our favorite topics include:
1. What did you do today?
2. What's the funniest thing that happened to you today?
3. What happened in the news?
4. What are our plans for next weekend?

If you have guests over, a good way to start a conversation is to find out where each person was a year ago, five years ago, ten years ago, and so forth, *on this day of the year.* Pretty soon, you'll be getting the story of everyone's life—and sharing the pertinent parts of yours too. Once that is done, you might talk about:

1. What makes you happy?
2. Where is the prettiest place you've been?
3. What's your favorite book, music, movie?
4. What are you doing now that you've never done before?

And just anything that comes to mind.

We're in the food business most of all. We're a place you can buy milk, bread, beef, chicken, tortillas, pasta, beans, and rice Cheaper! than at the biggest stores in town. We have the basics for a fancy meal made from scratch at low everyday prices, but we also have some quick and easy meals that a new homemaker can start out with. If you're just getting started at having a nice dinner, it's better to make a simple dinner well than to be tired and cranky from a huge production that isn't just right. Practice makes perfect!

Some of the material in this bagatorial was taken from *The Amy Vanderbilt Complete Book of Etiquette: A Guide to Contemporary Living,* by Letitia Baldrige (New York: Doubleday, 1978). You may also want to look at *Emily Post's Etiquette,* by Elizabeth Post (New York: HarperCollins, 1992)—originally written in 1922, the Post guide is a commensense view of manners for an ordinary person who wants to show consideration for others. Also recommended: "Behavior," from "The Conduct of Life," by Ralph Waldo Emerson, and *Management in the Home,* by Lillian Gilbreath, who raised fifteen children—graciously.

Get Rich by Saving!

Do You Want to Be Rich?

Sure, you say you want to be rich, but do you really want to be rich? Are you willing to follow a few rules that will ensure that you become wealthy?

Most People Do Not Control Their Own Destiny

Most people work to earn enough money to pay this month's bills from next month's paycheck. Financial dependence breeds unhappiness and resentment. It doesn't have to be that way. You can change if you just save part of what you make. A wise man said, "Cash is your best friend. . . . It allows you to live your life without intimidation."

Statistics show that nineteen out of twenty people who reach the age of sixty-five are without adequate funds to support themselves—and must rely on an unsure Social Security system and the charity of their still-producing families for their livelihood.

Don't Let This Happen to You!

It's so easy to be in the top 5 percent of the wealthy class of the United States. You only need to learn and practice these three rules:

Rule #1:
The rule of the nine-tenths. This is the primary rule. If you live it, you will become wealthy. It doesn't matter how much or how little you make. You just set aside and save one-tenth of what you make.

Rule #2:
The rule of controlled spending. You must limit your spending to nine-tenths of what

you earn. You need to recognize and remember that, even if you spend every dollar you earn gratifying your desires, you will not satisfy all of your desires. Millionaires have as many unsatisfied desires as you.

Rule #3:

The rule of one-tenth and its increase. You must put the one-tenth of your income that you save to work. You can't work your way to wealth, you can only save and invest your way. If you work twenty-four hours a day, you'll never earn enough to be wealthy. Your savings and their earnings have to do it for you.

This Is an Example of How Saving and Investing Work

If you save just $1,000 each year and invest it at 10 percent interest, you have $2,100 in two years. You'll have $16,000 after ten years. If you start saving at the age of thirty, you'll have $271,000 when you retire at the age of sixty-five. You'll have $542,000 if you save $2,000 a year.

Make yourself the promise that you'll start today. Gain control of your life and your destiny. Let cash become your best friend. Save some money today.

What We Know

Here is a lot of experience. We boiled it down to a few expressions. Does it matter who said it first or who said it best? What matters now is whether or not it makes sense to you.

1. Do unto others as you would have them do unto you.

2. Solve your own problems first. Many want to start helping others before they stop being part of the problem. Do something about improving the things you own. Take care of your own situation before worrying about everybody else.

3. It's good to help other people. If you want to give something away or help somebody, make sure you are doing it with your own money and effort.

4. If you want to help, first help those you know. Help yourself. Help your family. Help your wife. Help your children. Help your employees. Help your neighbors.

5. Brighten your own corner. Do good in areas you know something about.

6. You own your body and you own what you acquire to sustain it. You are never broke as long as you are alive. It's the basic property right and the most valuable thing in the world. We all have boundaries. It's wrong to cross other people's boundaries. It's wrong for them to cross yours.

7. You only own what you own. Most people think they own a lot of things they don't own.

8. You are what you are. Be happy with it. Satisfaction is something different.

9. You have options about your quality of life. You have a choice about how you will live and at what level you will live.

10. Never give a customer a reason to go elsewhere.

11. You must develop financial discipline. Innovation without financial discipline is like building on quicksand.

12. Cash is your best friend. It allows you to live without intimidation.

13. It's important to own real estate. The landlord always wins in the long run. Owners of real estate without mortgages are among the most difficult people to deal with.

14. You receive in the same manner as you spend. Why this is true is hard to explain.

15. People are the most important factor in business. Ask: "Are these people I can do business with?" If the answer is anything other than yes, reject the deal no matter how attractive it otherwise appears.

16. No one hires well. The sin is keeping people after you know you made a hiring mistake. The people who work for you know which employees should be let go. Don't disappoint them. On the other hand, don't throw away competence. And be honest: if employees are really your biggest asset, how much can you get when you sell an employee?

17. If you are selling things, hire optimists. Enthusiasm is catchy. Business runs on optimism. You don't have to make something to sell it. In fact, find out if you can sell it before you make it.

18. It's a lot easier to buy than to sell. You don't know how tough life is until you have to sell something. Selling teaches you reality. You get a lot more Christmas cards when you buy than when you sell.

19. In most organizations there is a responsible person who cares about that business. If you have a problem, keep going up the chain of command until you find that person. If you find no one cares, write off the organization.

20. If you look at the odds, you'll bet on sin to beat virtue. Sin seems free, but virtue appears expensive.

21. Develop a frame of reference. To operate without a frame of reference is very difficult. To operate with an unrealistic frame of reference is dangerous. Everyone needs a philosophy. Fit your philosophy to reality with logic. Then be a zealot until you're sure you're wrong.

22. Point of view is very important. Perspective is worth eighty points on the IQ scale.

23. The last movie you saw, the last book you read, the last record you bought shape your understanding of the world. Be wary of people who haven't seen a movie since *The Sound of Music.*

24. Curiosity is the most underrated quality. People who want to know everything are worth a lot more than people who think they know enough. It isn't always fun, but you can find out a lot by asking questions. People like to talk about themselves.

25. All of us are dumb, but not in the same places.

26. Analyze everything. Progress comes from connecting two unrelated thoughts.

27. If you're losing, change the rules. Play by rules that make sense to you here and now.

28. Problems are never insolvable. When faced with a gigantic problem, look at it carefully and analyze the cracks. Overcome it or go around it by handling the pieces of the problem you already understand.

29. No number is monolithic. It's only the sum of the parts. Don't believe a number you didn't make up yourself.

30. Don't believe hype. Acceptance is rarely related to merit. Success happens. Hype helps. Hype sells. Don't underestimate hype. Take advantage of hype when you can. Be skeptical and cynical for your own good. It's particularly dangerous when the guy spreading hype believes his hype. Most of what you hear every day starts as a press release. Unfortunately, a lot of hype goes into our frame of reference.

31. You don't live in a meritocracy. You fool yourself if you believe you are judged and receive benefits based on arbitrary rules and standards.

32. It takes a lot of learning to realize one doesn't have to have an opinion on every subject. You don't have to attend every fight to which you're invited.

33. What's the present value of perfect knowledge? Smart people decide with fewer clues. When the wise man does some thinking, the fool does some thinking too.

34. You do better when you keep score in numbers. The danger is that keeping score in numbers can make you a small person.

35. Wealth and success strike like lightning. The world looks for reasons and rules to live by to become rich and famous. There are lots of reasons people do well. The best way is to be in the right place and the right business at the right time. Sometimes success just happens. Don't try to explain why lightning strikes where it does. Know that chance favors the prepared mind.

36. The ability to say "no" now and then makes you successful. The less you must say "yes," the greater your chances for success.

37. Successful people do what unsuccessful people are afraid to do.

38. He who builds no castles in the air will have none upon the sands.

39. When you think you can no longer be busted out of the game, you can be corrupted quickly. Nothing is more vulnerable than entrenched success.

40. Self-made men usually make their mouths too large.

41. An entrepreneur is someone who lifted the calf and can't spell the word.

42. An optimist is a person who thinks he can afford to retire.

43. A business must have a fundamental advantage to be successful. It has to be based on a concept. Concepts have lives. The lucky learn a concept early. The smart change the way they use a concept before the dumb people accept it. Know where you stand on a concept's time scale. Position yourself to change the concept, to make the concept obsolete, before someone else changes it first and leaves you behind. There is enough money and brains around to make almost any concept obsolete before it has repaid all the costs incurred. You lead for as long as other operators think you're crazy. When they stop believing you're crazy, the market becomes saturated.

44. A trend in motion continues until it actually stops. The direction of the tide is very important. Even strong swimmers drown when swimming against the tide.

45. You can decide at what level you want to operate.

46. Price counts. If you want a business of any size, it's going to be in the price market. It's terrible to teach a child that price isn't number one.

47. If you can do things a little bit better and a little bit cheaper than the other guy, you probably have a pretty good business. Unfortunately, you can't choose one. You need to do them both.

48. Growth is intergenerational. Live with the idea that you must help your children become better off than you are. Inheritance may not be fair, but it's far better than any other method. The world progresses through intergenerational growth in both culture and riches. It's important

to live so you leave something of value behind when you go, such as money, values, reputation, and philosophy.

49. Competence is independent of heritage. Each generation must develop its own competence.

50. There are few lessons you can teach a child more important than the lesson of compound interest.

51. Develop a goodwill bank with everybody you know. Make regular deposits of goodwill to maintain a positive balance in each account.

52. You should try to earn more this year than you earned last year.

53. Family members should treat each other with the same courtesy and deference as they treat their friends.

54. There is always someone who has something bigger, better, and brighter than you have.

55. Ugly is fair to the lover.

56. Never sleep with a person who has more problems than you.

57. Fidelity in marriage is a practicality. Many don't know this. It costs them.

58. Bring at least five topics to every party.

59. Racism is selective remembering and selective forgetting.

60. Life isn't fair, but you can be fair by your own rules.

61. Relationships are reciprocal. If you don't like someone, that someone won't like you. If you think you've fooled someone, you've fooled yourself. No deal can stand without future adjustments. Both sides have to change a bit and give a little.

62. Only play on two-way streets. Don't deal with people who refuse to compromise. Get out of relationships that are all one-way. Relationships can never be validated until both parties put something at risk. Don't play in a game where the other person has nothing at stake. The rule of the world is "If it's free, take it." You don't know the value of a thing unless the other person has to give up something he or she values to obtain it. Always have an entry fee. Demand is infinite at zero cost. Separate true believers from rice Christians.

63. No one takes care of property as well as an owner. That which everyone owns, everyone violates. This is the tragedy of the commons.

64. We need to know the value people place on things. That's why market pricing is so important. It's why we must encourage capitalistic acts between consenting adults.

65. Most people will believe what you want them to believe so long as you pay them. If you pay them a lot, they won't even care if it doesn't make sense.

66. Think of the *Titanic*. When your ship starts sinking, you will be surprised by who stays on the deck with you instead of running to the lifeboats.

67. One must put a lot of messages in a lot of bottles to communicate. It's ineffective, but often it's the only way.

68. We suffer most from the poverty of desire.

69. Profit is a small price to pay for efficiency. People tell you they are with a nonprofit organiza-

tion as if that's a mark of virtue. How do they know if their results are worth anything to anybody?

70. The rich are getting richer and the poor are getting poorer. The beauty of capitalism is that you can choose which group to be in. The ranks of the rich and the poor include different people all the time.

71. The rich man needs to know how the poor man feels, and the poor man needs to know how hard the rich man works.

72. There is a cost to everything. That's why every choice is a tradeoff.

73. Life is tough on the prairie, and only the fittest survive. You live in a cruel universe. Don't fool yourself.

74. Actions have consequences.

75. It's okay to make mistakes. Amateurs don't know this, and it paralyzes them. It's OK to be wrong 50 percent of the time. Let your good decisions run, and change your bad decisions as soon as you know they are bad.

76. Get information to the part of the brain that takes action. Knowledge isn't worth much without action.

77. Find what works. There are magic buttons. Find magic buttons to things that are worth doing. Magic buttons don't always have to make sense or be explainable.

78. Live your life so you can identify and declare a victory.

79. Do things a little bit better every day.

80. Tell the truth in all matters, no matter how bizarre it is. Most people won't believe you anyway, so your secrets are safe. Nothing is more secret than a revealed secret.

81. People are living longer. Live your life as if you expect to live to be 150 years old. Older people are beginning to say, "I'd have taken better care of myself if I knew I was going to live this long."

82. Rich men can be foolish longer than poor men. This may give you time to correct your mistakes.

83. It's wrong to use force or fraud. It's wrong for a group of people to do what it's wrong for a person to do as an individual. If one takes care of the means, the end takes care of itself.

84. We have 1,231 more state laws in 1992 than we had in 1991. That brings the number of new state laws to 15,415 for the last ten years. Do people behave better?

85. There ought *not* to be a law. Coercion doesn't make anyone do anything. People who obey laws don't need the law to tell them right from wrong.

86. You have less freedom every time a planning commission meets. You have less freedom every time a city council operates. You have less freedom every time a legislative body convenes.

87. Some people are as addicted to forcing other people to do things as others are to alcohol and narcotics. The use of laws to attempt to change human behavior is more dangerous than any other addictions.

88. There isn't any hope in reversing the trend to statism until some of us are willing to refuse to accept bribes from the government. The smallest club in the world is composed of those who don't accept Social Security. The government has no money of its own. It only has what it takes from you and me.

89. Fascism in the name of environmentalism is still fascism. Environmental fascism is one of the current threats to our freedom.

90. Capitalistic and democratic planners can't plan any better than communist or fascist planners. The world is too complex to be planned by governments. People become better off when all of us, as owners of ourselves and our own property, do what we can with our own bodies and our own property.

91. We manage water in California in the same way communists managed whole economies. That's why our bountiful supplies of water are misused.

92. There is a time in every person's life when he must quit blaming others and take control of his own life. The earlier this happens to a person, the happier he, his family, and his friends will be.

93. Life is never going to be perfect. Nothing is going to solve all the problems of the world. It isn't going to come out right for everyone. Bad things happen to good people all the time.

94. How can we hope to solve difficult problems when we can't solve the traffic problem? Each day hundreds of thousands of people sit in gridlock. Men will suffer that which is sufferable. Use the market to decide the sensible use of roads.

95. We need more capitalism rather than more democracy. We need more respect for individual choice and individual rights.

96. Some rejoice because people consume less liquor, beer, and wine. Truth is that a significant number of would-be alcohol users have switched to drugs. You won't read this in your newspaper.

97. Drugs must be decriminalized. The war on drugs has failed, and not for lack of effort nor for lack of money.

98. Police make reports and provide retribution at monopolistic prices. Nobody protects anything by relying on the police.

99. Don't let government become the most important thing in your life. Realize you must take control of your life and solve your own problems. Do nothing to pay homage or aggrandize public officials. The pageant of government is performed to transfer power and authority from the individual to the government.

100. Organizations are run for the benefit of their operators. This is true of all organizations, including government, businesses, and nonprofit groups.

101. Leave all your rules, advice, adages, strategies, and opinions open-ended. You will change them as you gain experience and knowledge.

WHAT WE KNOW

Powerful Forces Want to Stop You from Driving. We Say:

Drive and Be Free!

by Pat Joyce

Two types of people talk about energy conservation: those who want to reduce their own consumption and those who want to reduce everyone else's consumption. The first group of people think about how to use energy wisely. The second group dream up ways to force other people to do their will.

An average American travels twenty miles on a gallon of gasoline. Many cars can double that mileage. A few cars almost triple that mileage. If saving energy is your sincere concern, you ought to be driving a high-mileage vehicle, such as the Honda Civic VX (48 mpg city, 55 mpg highway) or the Geo Metro (45 mpg city, 50 mpg highway).

If the United States fleet average fuel rate improved to 40 mpg, we'd use half as much gasoline as we do now. Think about it. If you want to be part of the solution, buy one of those cars. Encourage your friends and family to do the same. Over the years, many Americans have made this choice.

Can't afford a new car? Well, at least you ought to check the pressure in your tires. Underinflated tires can cut your mileage by 6 percent. Lighten the load while you're at it. A hundred pounds in the trunk cuts a half-mile off a gallon. And get a tune-up! A car out of tune will cost you more to fuel than the cost of the tune-up.

Still in love with high gas taxes? Think the Europeans figured it out? Look at these charts.

We're in a bigger country, snort tax advocates! We have more roads! Well, Americans also have a lot lower taxes—for now. There are 144,275,000 cars registered in the United States. Tax advocates scheme to get more dollars from each one.

Powerful forces in the United States want to restrict your freedom. They want to force you to use buses and other public-transit methods. These people *know* you are incapable of making your own decisions. Some are sham "environmentalists" who claim to speak for nature. Some say they worry about America's strategic position since it imports petroleum. Many realize *their* ends require a restriction in the private use of automobiles. These people are addicted to wanting to make choices for you.

Ask a regular guy what will happen to him if the price of gasoline increases by 50 cents per gallon. Will he drive less? You bet! Will some people be forced to stop driving? Yes, even to the point where more families won't even have a car. Will some have to quit their jobs or move to another home because they can't afford to commute? Yes. Increased gas taxes make the country poorer—and it hurts the average working man a lot more than it hurts the urban bureaucrat, the college professor, or the affluent politician.

Let's try to keep our freedom of choice. Freedom to drive where we want, when we want, in what we want, is a more precious freedom than most realize. Those who want to raise taxes, to restrict driving, and to legislate "energy solutions" oppose your right to live how you want to live, to go where you want to go, to see who you want to see, and to do what you want to do.

Brighten the corner where you are! Control your own consumption, first. When people worry about the "energy crisis," make sure they're practicing what they preach. Then, when they advocate higher taxes, make sure they realize it's a freedom issue—even at a penny a gallon. These folks ought to run their own lives.

An average American driver used 508 gallons of gasoline in 1989. Western states' drivers use more gasoline, historically, because they must travel farther. At California's current rate of about 37.9 cents per gallon, the average American pays $192.50 in gas taxes per year. California collects $5,110,839,000 in direct gasoline taxes each year.

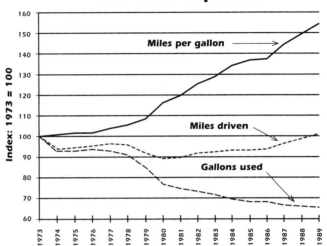

Cars Have Improved

Source: Energy Information Administration, Monthly Energy Review, May 1991, which is prepared from Department of Transportation, Fereral Highway Administration, Federal Highway Statistics Division. 1973 through 1985: Highway Statistics Summary to 1985, Table VM-201A; 1986 forward: Highway Statistics, Table VM-1.

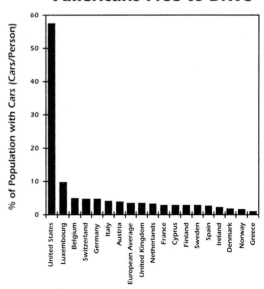

Americans Free to Drive

Foreign Tax Slaves

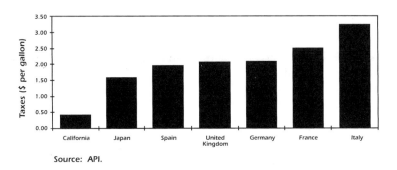

Taxes ($ per gallon)

California | Japan | Spain | United Kingdom | Germany | France | Italy

Source: API.

Each additional 5 cents in gas taxes per gallon costs the average American $25.40 more. In California as a whole, that's $134,486,485 more in taxes, plus $10,422,702 more in state sales taxes. California's gasoline taxes are even higher than they seem, thanks to the sales tax. This state is one of only nine states with a tax-on-a-tax.

Anti-car, protax propaganda has convinced many that to drive is bad and that gas taxes don't hurt. Stop the guilt and fight the taxes!

Taxation is waste. We all know that. Increasing gasoline taxes just fuels the monster. Who believes increased gas taxes will mean better roads? Government is so paralyzed, so immobilized by regulation and bureaucracy, that nothing gets accomplished. Two years after the '89 quake, the Cypress Freeway in Oakland, the Embarcadero in San Francisco, and parts of San Francisco's central freeway wait to be rebuilt or replaced. As of this writing, there isn't even an acceptable plan!

Gas taxes were once collected to build better highways. That's no longer so. When federal gasoline taxes increased to 14 cents a gallon (and diesel taxes to 20¢ per gallon), only half the revenues went into the highway trust fund. The other half was earmarked for "deficit reduction." (*San Francisco Examiner*, April 23, 1991.)

Gasoline taxes are popular with some people because they figure the oil companies pay the taxes. The truth is that oil companies pass the taxes on. Users pay all taxes. If you drive, you pay gas taxes. If you buy anything from a business that uses a car, you pay gas taxes in a roundabout way. If taxes increase, Cheaper! stores will collect more for the state. You'll have less freedom to

California Gasoline Use, 1952–89

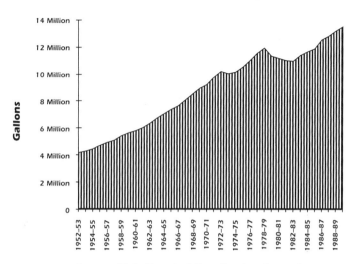

Gallons

14 Million
12 Million
10 Million
8 Million
6 Million
4 Million
2 Million
0

1952–53 1954–55 1956–57 1958–59 1960–61 1962–63 1964–65 1966–67 1968–69 1970–71 1972–73 1974–75 1976–77 1978–79 1980–81 1982–83 1984–85 1986–87 1988–89

**Source: State Board of Equalization Annual
Report 1989–90.**

So Taxes Skyrocket

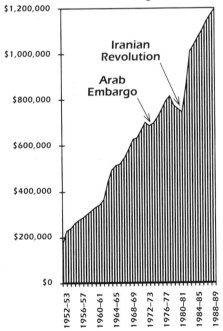

$1,200,000
$1,000,000
$800,000
$600,000
$400,000
$200,000
$0

Iranian
Revolution

Arab
Embargo

1952–53 1956–57 1960–61 1964–65 1968–69 1972–73 1976–77 1980–81 1984–85 1988–89

**Source: State Board of Equalization
Annual Report, 1989-90.**

When You Buy Gasoline

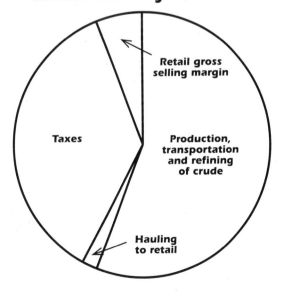

Retail gross
selling margin

Taxes

Production,
transportation
and refining
of crude

Hauling
to retail

spend as you please. The more taxes you pay, the less money you have to spend productively.

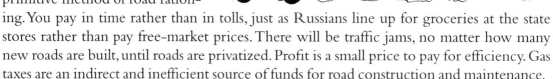

So how to solve gridlock on the highway? Traffic jams are a primitive method of road rationing. You pay in time rather than in tolls, just as Russians line up for groceries at the state stores rather than pay free-market prices. There will be traffic jams, no matter how many new roads are built, until roads are privatized. Profit is a small price to pay for efficiency. Gas taxes are an indirect and inefficient source of funds for road construction and maintenance.

Higher gas taxes won't drive Cheaper! stores out of business. Gas taxes just hurt customers. Gasoline retailing continues to become more efficient in California. Gasoline taxes account for almost 40 cents per gallon. Total wholesale and retail distribution costs are less than 10 cents per gallon. Gasoline selling margins are only a small part of our total margin. It's the principle that counts.

We'll survive because we're going to have fewer competitors in the gasoline business. In 1971, the state Board of Equalization issued 22,431 service-station permits. In 1991, the board issued just 10,708 permits. That's down by 530 permits from 1990! Half the surviving stations will be out of business in ten years. To survive, a station will have to meet stringent and expensive regulations. Our stores already have the double contained (a quarter-inch of steel surrounded by a quarter-inch of steel, coated with fiberglass and continuously electronically monitored) underground storage tanks that will be mandated by the end of the decade. We also have one of the most efficient methods to sell gasoline. Our competitors will have to make a substantial investment to catch up to us.

Gasoline taxes are too high already. Feel outraged, not guilty. We all need to say it over and over: "No new taxes! No new taxes! No new taxes!" Reduce government spending! Speak up! Spend your own money and your own time as you see fit. Let us know what you think.

What Is a "Business"?

by Lemuel R. Boulware

Whether we realize it or not, most of us get some or all our living from the business in our community.

Just what do we mean by a "business"? Do we mean an "it," or an inanimate "thing," or money, or goods, or machinery, or stock certificates, or the "few"? No!

A business is people—the many—who come together voluntarily to help each other do many times more toward supplying customers with an attractive value in a desired product or service than they each could do alone, with the aid only of the ideas, facilities, and human contacts each producer could himself or herself supply.

What makes it mostly possible for them to do so much more is the way investors and managers have provided the arm-lengthening ideas, designs, materials, facilities, coordination, volume, subdivision or operations, opportunity for specialization, broad market contacts, and risk-taking ability and willingness.

These people come together to do voluntarily their part as contributors—and to cash in their resulting claims—on a something-for-something basis. They do so in these five roles:

1. As *investors* who have voluntarily risked their savings in the hope—but not the certainty—that they will be adequately rewarded for making possible the arm-lengthening facilities which, in essense, are what a business offers its participants.

   The important fact here is that the investor believe an adequate incentive is there in the beginning and is continuing. Any time the customer favor enjoyed by the business weakens, or internal cooperation falters, or there is unfavorable influence from outside, this incentive for the investor to support the operation will diminish or disappear. This will do great harm to both the investor and the other four participants.

   For the risk and use of the investor's funds, the return has varied widely from total loss to a high percentage of gain. But for the businesses which have long survived, the return has varied roughly between 4 percent and 6 percent of the sales dollar.

2. As *customers* who give employees and others their daily work to do in return for being offered values attractive enough to make these customers want to buy.

   A ridiculous impression has been growing in this country that a business can voluntarily—or under force—supply its employees with job security. A business's investors may have provided facilities to do certain work (a) if there is such work to do and (b) if the business offer is best. But if its customers have no work they desire done or believe better offers are available by competitors, the employer will not be able to offer work.

3. As *suppliers* who furnish from outside that part of the work which they can do better or more economically—or both—than can be done at that time inside the business. They can sell at a price lower than the business cost and yet make a profit, because of volume, or specialized efficiency, or a better business climate. With new low-cost suppliers becoming available in areas like Asia and Mexico, it behooves a business to keep constantly alert to the opportunities offered—for two reasons: one is to do right by its customers and the other is to be sure to keep aware that one's competitors have access to these same superior opportunities.

4. As *employees* who do the work which can be done better or more economically inside the given business.

   Both the employer and employee have to keep in mind that every job is in competition every minute with the values offered in outside finished-product or component suppliers. This competition is in the employee's output of skill, care, and effort from his inner resources, for which he can expect the going market price in pay benefits, and opportunity for advancement.

5. As *neighbors* who determine whether or not there will be the tax and regulation policies, the protection of person and property, and the enlightened cooperation needed for the business to be able to attract sales and otherwise be useful. In return, the neighbors want business to bring money into town, supply jobs, provide sales to local suppliers, protect or increase the value of homes, and directly or indirectly support the merchants, schools, churches, charitable institutions, cultural projects, and environment preservation.

Obviously, a single adult may at one and the same time be an investor, customer, employee, and neighbor to a given business.

Just as obviously, it behooves every participant to strive voluntarily to help the business be conducted the nearest possible to the balanced best interests of all participants across their single and multiple roles—and to have each participant deservedly believe that this is so.

Capitalism

We are capitalists. Capitalism occurs when a willing buyer meets a willing seller. In capitalism, people must agree on prices for goods and services as they trade. When each person decides how much of his energy or the fruits of his energy will be spent to attain something he wants and does not have, that is capitalism.

We believe in the freedom of capitalistic acts between consenting adults. Free markets, without restraints, benefit mankind. Men who trade freely benefit themselves, and en masse, benefit each other. As Adam Smith wrote,

> Every individual necessarily labors to render the annual revenue of the society as great as he can. He generally indeed neither intends to promote the public interest, nor knows how much he is promoting it. . . . He intends only his own gain, and he is in this, as in many other cases, led by an invisible hand to promote an end which was no part of his intention. . . . By pursuing his own interest he frequently promotes that of the society more effectually than when he really intends to promote it. I have never known much good done by those who affected to trade for the public good.
>
> —*The Wealth of Nations,* 1776, book IV, chapter 2

Profit Is Essential

Profit is the difference between the money you take in and all your costs. Your costs include merchandise, materials, rent, salaries, utilities, taxes, advertising, repairs, interest, and a lot of other things. Pay all of them and what's left is profit. Profit is the cost of the future.

Profit is a difficult, poorly understood product of capitalism. Businesses must make a profit to survive. Businesspeople are forced to be realistic about what people will pay for goods and services. Profits are earned from what people actually do, not what they say they will do. Success in business is usually about what you must do, not what you want to do. Profits link activity to reality.

Profit is the price paid for investment. If profits are earned, more investments can and will be made. With profits, future opportunities are much more likely. Without investment, there is no business. Profit is the cost of capital. If profits attract capital, improvements are made. Efficient and profitable businesses attract capital and become big businesses. Big businesses stay big if profits are reinvested in profitable endeavors. For any business, profits are the insurance premiums against tomorrow's risks.

Profits are made despite competition. If profits appear to be high, competitors cut prices to get profit for themselves. Those who are profitable have been efficient. Businesses grow to become big businesses when they have been both efficient and profitable.

Profit is a small price to pay for efficiency. Nonprofit organizations are an excuse for inefficiency and plunder. The world's rule is "For Free, Take." Nonprofit organizations don't have to find out if people are willing to give something up to get the product or service. No one cares about efficiency because no one is making any profit from the endeavor. If you find someone concerned about efficiency in a nonprofit organization, what you have is a business concealed behind a favorable tax status.

Profitable businesses satisfy demands in the market better than other alternatives. Without efficiency, without competition, without consumer satisfaction, without capital reinvestment, without *profit,* our lives would be solitary, poor, nasty, brutish, and short. Love your family? Go make a profit.

It Could Happen to You!

How to Write a Grocery Bag

The purpose of our company is to get and keep customers. We run a chain of grocery stores with prices cheaper than our toughest competitors. The bagatorials began when we realized that a lot of people like something to chew on when they buy their groceries.

It's all very logical. One day, John Roscoe was stuck in traffic at the toll plaza for the Benicia Bridge (over the Sacramento River) and he started thinking about the word "gridlock." Running a good store takes a lot of work, so we think about stores all the time. Cigarettes are a very important part of the grocery business. John wondered if "Gridlock" could make it as a cigarette brand name.

John has worked to be able to do what he wants to do. He persuaded Philip Morris to manufacture a private-label cigarette under the name "Gridlock." Private-label saves people a lot of money over the national brand. If you're going to beat the prices of the biggest stores in town, you can't afford to spend very much on advertising, but you can use all the ways at hand to deliver a message. We were going to buy grocery bags anyway, so we put an advertisement for Gridlock cigarettes on the bags.

When the bag came out, a reporter called. They'd found a line on the bottom of the bag. "Concerned about the effects of traffic stress on your life? Write to the Committee to Abolish Tolls . . ." it read. Newspapers, radio stations, and television ran stories on these interesting grocery bags. Unfortunately, the bags were printed before the cigarettes were manufactured, and we were too chagrined to tell reporters that we were advertising a product that was yet to be made.

This was in 1988. George Bush was running for president against Michael Dukakis. You know that, if you were hiring someone for an important position, you'd certainly use a better selection system than campaign primaries. No matter what system you used, if your finalists came out looking like George Bush or Michael Dukakis, you'd realize that your process was fundamentally flawed and you'd start from scratch. "George, Mike, thanks, but we've decided to keep looking," you'd say. And you'd start over.

But that's not why we printed "Don't Vote! It Only Encourages Them" on a grocery bag. Lord Acton was right: power corrupts. The federal government has tremendous power.

It's going to exercise that power regardless of how you vote. That power is used for purposes almost completely opposite to what the founders said they intended in the Preamble to the U.S. Constitution. Those who vote, even those who vote as a protest, each give their own sanction to the burgeoning power of the state.

People react strongly to this message. Several dozen people said they would never shop in our stores again. "We're sorry to hear that," we replied. "I hope you'll buy something from us again when it's to your advantage." Many people went to the stores to get a copy of this bagatorial. They noticed our prices, and sales increased. One lady sent us a gift subscription to *The Nation*.

Once you've experienced publicity and its effect on sales, you want to get some more. So we printed the Declaration of Independence on a bagatorial. And, to make it interesting, we added a headline: "Smash the State," it read. "Government Is for Slaves! Free Men Govern Themselves."[1]

People were furious. They said we were communists. They told us to go to Russia. They accused us of being poor writers. Some coward from the Posse Commitatus sent us an anonymous death threat. Our chief financial officer became hysterical. "This will cost my husband his security clearance!" she shrieked. We patiently pointed out that this text was the Declaration of Independence. We could sense the strain of tremendous cogitation. So we laughed.

After that it's been the story of the Emperor's New Clothes over and over again. We read a lot of books, newspapers, and magazines. We watch TV. We listen to talk radio. You probably do the same. We are skeptical about almost everything, because we are merchants. When we buy, we worry about whether we're getting the right price and quality. When we sell, we must persuade the customers that we're giving them a better deal than they can get from our toughest competitors.

You know as a customer that things ain't necessarily so. News is like that too. Strange things happen to us in business—like redevelopment—and we try to find out what's happening. There are a lot of people who are able to take what they want without paying for it. Nice news stories are crafted to conceal these scams. If you're working on a local news story, thinking about the logic and the facts could be extremely detrimental to your continued employment, so most reporters working a local beat force themselves to stop thinking. They go with the flow.

Working people, property owners, and businesses are the targets of these scams, so we find ourselves forced to find the facts and to think through the logic. Jay Chapman, who serves as our director of bureaucratic interfacing, finds a lot of figures for us. He searches out old books and he calls complete strangers to get the facts. We like to use numbers, because, even though we never believe a number we haven't made up by ourselves, you must know the numbers to know the story.

After you've checked the facts and thought it through, a bagatorial demands to be written. It seems pretty easy. What's going on? you ask. Why is it happening? You write the idea down on a piece of paper. You make a vow to yourself that you're going to make it the best thing you ever wrote. You are going to straighten everybody out. "Let the truth be known," you say to yourself. Ideas keep coming, and so pretty soon you have a file folder on the subject. The folder is full of clippings and notes and letters and copies. Writing is just a matter of stitching the facts together with logic.

Here's the problem: Pretty soon you have a lot of file folders on a lot of subjects. When you look up, your outrage fades and you go back to your business.

Our rule has always been "Business First, Bagatorials Second." We sell groceries and we give away bags. We serve 120,000 customers per day. Here's our special problem: Most customers want their groceries put into a grocery bag. We print between a million and two million copies of each bag. Printing a story on a bag costs practically nothing more than the cost of the bag itself, and these days our customers expect it. If we shut up, we might sell less! So, when Sally Baldwin tells us that she must order bags next Wednesday, our priorities reverse. It's time to turn a good idea into something sensible.

It's easy to have an opinion. It's easy to talk about something. It's difficult to write down a cogent position. Most of what we write is contrary to the established wisdom, but persuasion is not our challenge. Stating the obvious in opposition to established opinion in a few words is a challenge. Most readers have enough good sense to realize whether your position is truth or nonsense. We try to challenge the opinions which are firmly held but poorly constructed. We try to punch a hole in the other guy's hype.

Our early efforts were horrible. We rewrite, we try to state the obvious even more directly than before. We rewrite a lot, both because we would each like the pride of authorship, and because we do not necessarily agree with each other. If you're going to write a good bagatorial, you must learn when to listen and when to ignore criticism.

It's very satisfying to write a good bagatorial. You know this when people write or call and say, "I knew that and I really appreciate you saying it." Many of these people have extensive experience. Bagatorials try to be about the good sense that most people have but often ignore. We try to keep people from suffering that which is sufferable. We urge them, we *goad* them to improve their lives and their fortunes. When someone else does well, we're happy.

Truth, justice, and freedom? We love them. We also know that we are never the last word. We think of our ancient family motto, carved on the family crest that was brought from Myrmidonia: *Der Humor über Alles.* Last week a man came into our Calistoga store and asked for a bagatorial. "Do you like to read them?" asked our assistant manager. "Oh yes," said the customer, "but I need to use this one as a garbage bag."

You know you're written a really good bagatorial when a local official reads it from the dais during a public meeting—with anger. The bagatorials are all about self-reliance, and that really bothers the typical politico.

The most extreme reactions are usually pricked by the illustrations. Robert Leighton has illustrated most of the bagatorials, but he rarely reads the text. About two years ago, we stopped sending him the finished product, because we were afraid it would affect the drawings. Instead, we call him up as if he was a short-order cook in a diner. We talk about a picture and what it could look like. We argue over drawings that haven't even been drawn. Two days later, the envelope arrives, and PRESTO—that's even better than what we had in mind.

None of this would have happened unless John Roscoe read Ayn Rand's *The Fountainhead* in 1974. Nor would it have occurred if John Roscoe hadn't met Bob LeFevre. Bob LeFevre was a man who made his living writing and speaking about individual liberty. To this day, John Roscoe describes himself as a "small el' libertarian." Ned Roscoe is either a capitalist or a liberal, depending on your point of view.

The bagatorials allow us to be very private people. Even our few friends know very little about us. You know, there are two ways to keep a secret:

Don't tell anybody

or

Be absolutely candid with everyone and no one will believe you.

We do both. Most reporters who read our bagatorials suspect that we're engaged in a cynical campaign to manipulate the media, so they ignore us. Writing is a trade, and so they're skeptical to hear that grocers write and rewrite these bagatorials. Even better than publicity is privacy. We are able to speak for ourselves to our customers.

We receive a lot of mail because of the bagatorials. Some people want to know who really writes the bagatorials. It ought to be obvious from the topics. We're interested in subjects that our customers suggest, but we're primarily interested in our business. James Cash Penney was the greatest American merchant. Others have tried to reinvent what Penney knew and practiced, including Sam Walton, who began his career working for Penney. Realizing this, we try to get our business as close as possible to the essentials of good retailing. And we write about it.

An avid reader who happened to be a highway patrolman led us to the story on the CHP. Since then we've written a lot about law enforcement, and so we've become more strict in how we enforce the law. We've also written about self-improvement, and so we've worked to reward our employees for self-improvement. We sent fifty couples on a luxurious cruise through French Polynesia in 1995. We'll do something even better in 1996. Above all, we try to follow the Golden Rule.

Writing a bagatorial is better than writing to your congressman. A good bagatorial leads to simple, obvious things that you can do by yourself for yourself. We write a lot about the government, but we don't worry about the government. We don't hate the government. We hate theft and we hate fraud, but we have to get things done to get and keep customers. Sometimes the bagatorials lead to conflict with public employees, and while we resent it, we know that there is a price to be paid for free speech. On the other hand, some good, conscientious public employees appreciate our positions (and our prices). We work pretty well with them.

Sometimes people contact us and demand equal access to put their piece on our bagatorials. "It's just not fair!" they whine. We paraphrase Liebling to say that we've got freedom of the press because we own a press. These calls are a little bit like having a personal radio talk show.

One man wanted to know how bagatorials turned into bagatorials. "We took what we had to say and we put it on what we had to hand out" was the reply.

"That reminds me of when I was a kid," he said. "There was a guy who had a hardware store. Every day he'd write what he had to say and he'd put it up in his windows. Everybody in the neighborhood talked about it." Then he paused.

"You know, I have a window," he said with amazement. "I could do that."

That's how you write a grocery bag. Find something interesting. Get some facts together. Look in the encyclopedia. Check *Bartlett's Familiar Quotations*. Look at the statistical abstract. Talk to people in the know. Separate truth from fiction. Write it down. Let people ridicule it. Rewrite it. Cut out the baloney. Read it aloud. When you've got something interesting, put a snappy headline on the top.

And then put it in your window. Take the heat. Talk to people. Then start over and do it again.

---

[1]Hardly anything we write is original. This was said by one of the defendants in the Haymarket Riot case.

About the Authors

John Roscoe grew up in Portland, Oregon. He graduated from Oregon State University during the Korean War. He enlisted in the United States Air Force, where he rose from enlisted to officer status. He opened his first store in 1957. John has studied the time-honored principles of successful retailing.

John, his wife Marilyn, his daughter Sally Baldwin, and Ned Roscoe operate a chain of nearly five hundred stores.

Ned Roscoe grew up in Walnut Creek, California. He graduated from the University of Chicago. He is a grocer. "My father is always write," he says. "And I am rewrite."